Popular
Thai
Cuisine

Popular Thai Cuisine

111 authentic and reliable recipes
for home-style cooking
with step-by-step illustrations

Edited by
Nidda Hongwiwat

SD BOOKS

Nidda Hongwiwat is a food writer. She is the founder and managing director of Sangdad Publishing Co., Ltd., a biggest cookbook publisher in Thailand. For the last 20 years she also serves as executive editor of Krua, a monthly magazine on food and culture, published by Sangdad. She has been writing numerous articles and books on food, nature cure, and gourmet travel.

Popular Thai Cuisine
ISBN 978-974-7588-37-8
First published in Thailand by
Sangdad Publishing Co., Ltd.
January 2003
Reprinted 2003, 2004, 2005, 2006, 2007, 2008, 2010, 2011, 2014, 2017
by SD Books, a registered trademark of Sangdad Publishing Co., Ltd.,
Copyrights © Sangdad Publishing Co., Ltd., 2003

Editor Nidda Hongwiwat **Recipe Consultant** Sisamon Kongpan **English Sub-Editors** Oranuch Wangsuekul, Rapeepan Jaipakdee, Chistopher J. Bruce **Recipe testing** Obchery Imsabai, Buppha Kittikul, Sirilak Rodyan **Photography & Design** Samart Sudto **Photography Assistant** Phinnasak Kaewyai, Soonthorn Keereerat **Layout** Woranad Phansue **Marketing Director** Nan Hongwiwat **Production Director** Jiranan Tubniam **Color Separation** Scan Art Tel. [662] 292-0279-80 **Printer** Pimdee Co., Ltd. Tel. [662] 803-2694-7 **Publisher and Distributor** Sangdad Publishing Co., Ltd. 320 Lat Phrao 94 [Town in Town] Wangthonglang, Bangkok 10310, Thailand. **Tel.** [662] 934-4414 ext.102-110 **Fax.** [662] 538-1499 **e-mail:** marketing@sangdad.com **www.sangdad.com www.facebook.com/sangdadpublishing**

foreword

There are at least two good reasons why we are proud of publishing the present English edition of Popular Thai Cuisine. It is one of the first few books on Thai food which adopted a step-by-step illustrated cooking, making it possible and convenient even for beginners to cook delicious Thai food. The recipes are authentically Thai because they were approved by a highly reputed Thai food expert, Ajarn Sisamon Kongpan, or else developed from prevailing home-style cooking in the families and the communities. More importantly, the recipes are true and reliable because they had been subjected to repeat tests.

For almost a year that our in-house recipe department staff had been working very hard in developing and testing recipes under close guidance of Ajarn Sisamon. The recipes were carefully edited, and step-by-step cooking illustrations prepared. Food styling and photography were done beautifully in our own studio.

The recipes are organized into major sections as starters and snacks, soups, salads, curries, meat and poultry, fish and seafood, vegetables, rice, noodles, and desserts. With this step-by-step illustrated cookbook, you will find gourmet Thai cooking right at your fingertips.

Nidda Hongwiwat
January 2003

contents

ingredients

The taste of Thai food comes mainly from the wide range of flavor ingredients. The blending of these ingredients contributes to the harmonious tastes unique for each dish. Besides, Thai cooking uses a lot of herbs and vegetables, regarded widely as "health food".

Fine Thai cooking starts with carefully selecting and using the right and fresh ingredients. The art of Thai cooking requires a good understanding of the primary ingredients as spices, herbs, and vegetables.

vegetables

Thai eggplants
Ma-kheua-praw
A greenish white ball-shaped eggplant with the same size as lime. Select only the young eggplants having thick flesh and less seeds.

Pea eggplants
Ma-kheua-phuang
A tiny green eggplant. Buy the ones with fresh skin and tightly packed in clusters.

Yard-long beans
Thua-fak-yao
Select only the fresh one which is crisp yet juicy in taste with green and firm pod.

Baby corns
Khao-phot-awn
Harvested from the special varieties of corn, it is sweet and crisp. The whole cob is used in cooking.

Angled loofahs
Buap-liam
An oblong, pointed, dark green with 10 longitudinal ridges to be peeled off before cooking. Select only young loofahs.

Kale
Kha-naa
The leathery green leave vegetables popular in Chinese dishes. Medium-sized kale gives crispy texture and no bitter taste.

Winged beans
Thua-phuu
The lively green rectangular-shaped pod with a fringe extension at each corner, the "wings" of the beans. Stale beans have black or rotten wings.

Swamp cabbages
Phak-bung
Sometimes called water convolvulus or Thai morning glory. There are 2 different kinds, the Thai and Chinese varieties.
The Chinese variety is larger and more tender when cooked.

Bean sprouts
Thua-ngawk
Three types of bean sprouts are used in Thai dishes. The first 2 types are harvested from green and black mung beans, while the third from soy beans.

Red spur chilies
Phrik-chee-faa-daeng
Select only those with fresh skin, thick flesh and green stems. The spur chili is generally carved, sliced or shredded and used as a garnish or added to curries and stir-fried dishes.

Yellow spur chilies
Phrik-chee-faa-lueang
It is hotter and smells stronger than the red and green varieties. Preferably used in chili paste, pickled chili in vinegar or added to spicy stir-fried dishes.

Hot chilies
Phrik-khee-nuu
Small but very hot chili. Use only ones whose fresh stems are still on.

Karen chilies
Phrik-ka-riang
A kind of hot chilies which is really hot. Buy the plump, firm and light red ones with fresh green stems.

Bell chilies
Phrik-yuak
Light green in color and mild in taste. Use those with glossy green skin, fresh stems, and no wrinkles.

Bell pepper
Phrik-waan
It has many colors: green, red, yellow and orange. Buy the ones with firm green stems and bright color.

Straw mushrooms
Het-faang
The budding mushrooms will have better taste than the blooming ones. Keep them in a cool dry place and wash just before cooking.

Angel mushrooms
Het-nang-faa
Looking similar to abalone and oyster mushrooms, but its color is off-white to light brown. The medium-sized mushrooms are the most preferable.

Shiitake mushrooms
Het-hawm
It is called fragrant mushroom in Thai. There are both fresh and dried varieties. For fresh shiitakes, buy ones which have thick caps and brown color.

Saw-leave coriander
Phak-chee-farang
With long narrow leaves and saw edges, it can be eaten fresh, added to spicy soup to reduce the fishy or meaty smell.

Coriander
Phak-chee
The plant is grown for its leaves, roots and seeds. Pick those with fresh light green leaves with roots on.

Spring onions
Ton-hawm
It is mostly used as a garnish in Thai dishes. Buy the ones with fresh green leaves and roots on.

Cucumbers
Taeng-kwaa
This small variety of cucumbers has the crispiest texture and sweetest taste.

Large cucumbers
Taeng-raan
Mature cucumbers have yellow skin, more seeds and less flesh. Keep the cucumber in a refrigerator or dry place, and wash just before using.

Lettuces
Phak-kaad-hawm
A kind of loosehead lettuce. Lettuce with fresh light green leaves is sweeter than the one with greener leaves.

Wax gourds
Fak-khiaw
Sometimes called a winter melon. The young gourd is small in size, while the mature one is bigger.

Cabbages
Ka-lum-plee
Can be eaten fresh with spicy salad or chili paste dip, and added in soup or stir-fried dishes.

Chinese celery
Khuen-chai
Having smaller stalks but stronger flavour than its western counterpart, Chinese celery is used to bring aroma to the food.

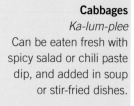

Limes
Ma-nao
Many varieties are available. Buy the ones with yellowish green thin skin.

Tomatoes
Ma-khua-thet
Large-sized tomato is generally used as a garnish or added to stir-fried dishes such as sweet & sour pork. The smaller one, cherry tomato, is used in papaya salad and curries.

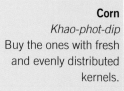

Corn
Khao-phot-dip
Buy the ones with fresh and evenly distributed kernels.

spices&herbs

Dried chilies
Phrik-haeng
Both spur and hot chilies are used. Dried hot chilies are normally roasted and ground, and used as the seasoning. While dried spur chilies are used mostly in curry paste.

Shallots
Hawm-daeng
The zesty small red onion. The ones with glossy purplish red skin give strong smell, while those with yellowish orange skin are sweeter in taste.

Onions
Hawm-yai
Good quality onions are heavy with dry and smooth skin. Keep them in a ventilated area or in a basket for longer use. Do not refrigerate.

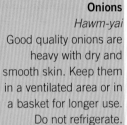

Garlic
Kra-thiam
Thai garlic has small cloves with rather soft skin but strong aroma. Hanging the garlic in a ventilated area helps extend its shelf life.

Galangal
Khaa
A member of the ginger family, it has pungency and tang, quite unlike that of the common ginger. Buy only young galangal with plump roots and pinkish white skin.

Ginger
Khing
Two forms are used in the Thai cooking, young ginger is usually sliced and sprinkled over steamed fish. The mature one with stronger flavour is best added to the sauces.

Lemon grass
Ta-khrai
Pick the ones with plump base and light purple in color. Peel away the outer bulb until the pinker insides appears.

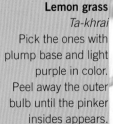

Kaffir limes
Ma-krut
A dark green herb that is valued for its zest and the unbeatable aroma of its leaf. The leaves are torn or sliced and added immediately to the dish to keep the strong aroma. The zest is sliced and pounded with the curry paste.

Coriander roots
Raak-phak-chee
A unique feature of Thai cooking is the use of coriander root to add aroma to various dishes.

Wild ginger
Kra-chai
The fresh plump roots have strong aroma and are juicy. Peel away the thin brown skin and wash thoroughly to reduce their strong flavour before cooking.

Holy basil
Ka-phrao
Two types are used in Thai cooking: green and purple red basil. The latter is more fragrant and spicier.

Mint
Sa-ra-nae
It is a fresh aromatic herb that cannot be missed in Thai spicy salad. Buy the fresh dark green leaves to get its full flavour.

Sweet basil
Ho-ra-phaa
The dark green leaves with red stems. Its leaves are slightly thicker than holy basil, and have own distinctive flavour.

Hairy basil
Maeng-lak
The thin hairy leaves with green stems have slightly weaker flavour than the sweet basil.

Turmeric
Kha-min
The one used in Thai cooking has carrot orange flesh and strong flavour. Placed in a plastic bag and keep refrigerated for longer use.

Green peppercorns
Phrik-thai-awn
The green or young peppercorns are flavourful but not too hot. The whole berries can be used, or lightly crushed to give more flavour.

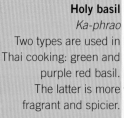

Coriander seeds
Luuk-phak-chee
The tiny round seeds with light brown skin. Wash, drain and roast until fragrant. Then pound finely and keep in an air-tight container.

Cumin
Yee-raa
The small elongated grayish white seeds resemble fennel in appearance. Wash, roast and pound or grind, then keep in a closed jar.

Cinnamon
Op-choey
The dark brown bark with spicy sweet flavour. Cinnamon is sold in the form of powder, flat sheet and stick. Wash and roast just before using for maximum fragrance.

Cardamom
Luuk-kra-waan
Each pod contains a dozen or so black seeds which are generally roasted, slit, pounded and added to the dish.

Nutmeg
Luuk-jan
A dark brown, egg-shaped seed. It is usually slit, roasted, ground and kept in an air-tight container.

Mace
Dawk-jan
The yellowish-brown, petal-like covering the seed. Mace is roasted, ground and best kept in an air-tight container.

Cloves
Kan-phluu
It is the bud picked before they flower and sun-dried to brownish black. The oil found in cloves is strong in flavour. Wash and roast until fragrant, can be used whole or ground.

Star anise
Poi-kak
The star-shaped fruit is an essential spice in Chinese five-spice powder. Wash and roast until fragrant before use.

Black pepper
Phrik-thai-dam
They are dried pepper berries with skin on. Mature berries are bigger in size and have stronger flavour.

White peppercorns
Phrik-thai-khao
Dried pepper berries with skin off. Select those with natural process of milling which produces the creamy rather than white berries.

Bay leaves
Bai-kra-waan
The dark green leaves used extensively in Western dishes. In Thai cooking, they are sometimes added to roast chicken and *mutsamun* curry.

Curry powder
Phong-karee
Spice mixture containing turmeric, coriander seeds, ginger, cloves, cinnamon, mustard, cardamom and others. It is the key ingredient in yellow curry paste, and also used in stir-fried crab dishes.

flour & noodles

Rice flour
Paeng-khao-jao
The dry flour has a coarser texture, and is used in most Thai desserts.

Glutinous rice flour
Paeng-khao-niaw
Commonly used in Thai desserts. There are 2 types available: black and white glutinous rice flour.

Mung bean flour
Paeng-thua-khiaw
Milled from hulled mung beans. It has smooth and soft texture, and becomes clear when cooked.

Arrowroot starch
Paeng-thao-yai-mom
Milled from arrowroots.
It gives the same texture as
the mung bean flour
when cooked.

Corn flour
Paeng-khao-pod
Normally corn flour is
used to thicken gravy
and sauces,
and sometimes added
to the stuffing.

Tapioca flour
Paeng-mun-sam-pa-lang
Made from tapioca,
or cassava tubers.
In Thai cooking, tapioca
flour is used to thicken
sauces.

Wheat flour
Paeng-saa-lee
2 types are
commonly used: normal
wheat flour and whole
wheat flour.

Mung bean noodles
Woon-sen
When cooked,
the noodles become
transparent.

Fermented rice vermicelli
Khanom-jeen
Thin round rice noodles,
sold fresh in the form of
wads. Rice vermicelli made
from fermented flour is
darker in colour and has
stronger flavour than
the one made from fresh
flour.

Chantaburi rice noodles
Kuai-tiaw-sen-jan
They are thin rice noodles
initiated from Chantaburi
Province. It is soft and
elastic, and is best for
stir-fried noodles. Pick the
ones of good quality,
no mold and not smelly.

Spring roll sheets
Paeng-paw-pia
A round spreadsheet
made from rice flour
batter. The freshly made
spring roll sheet is
tender and fragrance.

seasoning

Fish sauce
Nam-plaa
The clear brown liquid extracted from fermented fish or shrimp.
Good quality fish sauce is clear and has no dregs.

Light soy sauce
See-iu-khao
The soy sauce used in these recipes is the Chinese type. The first extracted soy sauce is tasty, fragrant and highly nutritious.

Seasoning sauce
Sauce-prung-ros
A seasoned soy sauce which adds more flavour to the dish than the regular soy sauce. Select the one with high protein content, no preservatives and not more than 20% salt added.

Dark soy sauce
See-iu-dam
There are 2 types sold in the market. The salty dark soy sauce comes from a longer period of fermenting soy beans, while the sweet dark soy sauce is the mixture of light soy sauce and molasses.

Oyster sauce
Nam-man-hoi
It is the thick brown sauce made from fresh oysters. It has salty sweet taste, and is normally use to marinate the meat or added to Chinese stir-fried dishes.

Sugar
Nam-taan-sai
There are bleached and unbleached sugar which give the same sweet in taste but different in colour. The unbleached one is light brown and has slightly stronger fragrance.

Palm sugar
Nam-taan-peep
Made from either the sap of the coconut palm or sugar palm. The latter produces the soft-sweet taste with stronger flavour.

Rock sugar
Nam-taan-kruat
Made from the same process as refined sugar but not being granulated. It is used in soup and some Chinese beverages.

Brown sugar
Nam-taan-sai-daeng
The unbleached cane sugar has high moisture content and strong aroma.

Salt
Kluea
Both sea salt and table salt are commonly used in the Thai cooking.

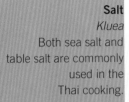

Chili sauce
Sauce-phrik
The mixture of chili and garlic seasoned with sugar, salt and vinegar. The level of spiciness-- mild, medium and extra hot-- can be chosen as preferred.

Vinegar
Nam-som-sai-chuu
Many types of vinegar are available in the market. Fermented vinegar is best for salad dressing, whereas distilled vinegar is suited for pickled vegetables.

Tamarind juice
Nam-ma-kham-phiak
Made from the mixture of tamarind flesh and water, and squeezed out the thick juice. It is added to the dishes to give a soft sour taste.

Fermented soybeans
Tao-jiaw
A mixture of fermented soybeans and flour. There are dark and light brown varieties depending on the length of brewing.

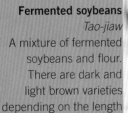

Shrimp paste
Ka-pi
Shrimps are salted, brewed for a time, allowed to dry and then ground to a paste. It has unique flavour and fragrance.

dried ingredients

Ground roasted rice
Khao-khua
It is sometimes called ground parched rice because the rice is soaked for a few minutes, drained and roasted over low heat until golden, then pound finely to powder.

Peanuts
Thua-li-song
It is commonly added to *mutsamun* curry, *phanaeng* dish, satay sauce and papaya salad. Good quality peanuts should have clean pale red soft shells, no mold or dirt.

White and black sesame seeds
Nga-khao, Nga-dam
It is preferably roasted over low heat until fragrant, lightly pound or crushed just before using as the stale roasted sesame seeds will have rancid smell.

Cashew nuts
Med-ma-muang-himaphaan
Available both whole and half seeds. Normally it is roasted or sautéed in small amount of oil over low heat until golden and done.

Dried shrimps
Kung-haeng
Various types are sold in the market. Buy the ones with natural orange in colour and not moist. For longer used, keep the dried shrimps refrigerated.

curry paste

Fried rice crackers
Khao-tang-thawt
It is the freshly cooked rice, spread evenly to form a round or rectangular shape, sun-dried and deep-fried in hot oil until lightly golden.

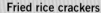

Red curry paste
Nam phrik kaeng phet

5 dried red spur chilies,
   seeded and soaked
5 shallots, sliced
10 cloves garlic
1 tsp galangal, finely sliced
1 tbsp lemon grass, sliced
1 tsp kaffir lime rind, finely sliced
2 tsp chopped coriander root
5 peppercorns
1 tbsp ground roasted coriander seed
1 tsp roasted cumin
1 tsp salt
1 tsp shrimp paste

• Pound together coriander seeds, cumin, and peppercorns to obtain a fine paste. Spoon onto a bowl and put aside.
• Pound dried chilies and salt thoroughly, add galangal, lemon grass, kaffir lime rind, coriander roots, garlic, shallots and pound well.
• Add the cumin mixture, follow with shrimp paste. Pound until everything is well-combined.

Green curry paste
Nam phrik kaeng khiaw waan

15 large green hot chilies
3 shallots, sliced
9 cloves garlic
1 tsp finely sliced galangal
1 tbsp sliced lemon grass
$1/2$ tsp finely sliced kaffir lime rind
1 tsp chopped coriander root
5 peppercorns
1 tbsp roasted coriander seeds
1 tsp roasted cumin
1 tsp salt
1 tsp shrimp paste

• Combine coriander seeds, cumin and peppercorn in a mortar, pound well. Transfer to a bowl and put aside.
• Pound hot chilies and salt together well. Add the remaining ingredients except shrimp paste, pound until mixed well.
• Add the cumin mixture and shrimp paste, continue pounding until smooth and fine.

Yellow curry paste
Nam phrik kaeng kari

3 large red spur chilies,
   seeded and soaked
5 roasted shallots
10 cloves roasted garlic
1 tsp galangal, finely sliced and roasted
1 tsp ginger, finely sliced and roasted
1 tbsp lemon grass, sliced
1 tbsp roasted coriander seeds
1 tsp roasted cumin
2 tsp curry powder
1 tsp salt
1 tsp shrimp paste

• In a mortar, pound coriander seeds and cumin together well. Transfer to a bowl and put aside. Peel roasted shallots and garlic, put aside.
• Pound dried chilies and salt together. Add ginger, galangal and lemon grass. Follow with roasted shallots, roasted garlic, cumin mixture, curry powder and shrimp paste. Pound well after each adding to obtain a fine paste.

Kaeng khua curry paste
Nam phrik kaeng khua

5 large dried red spur chilies,
   seeded and soaked
10 shallots, sliced
20 cloves garlic
1 tsp finely sliced galangal
1 tbsp sliced lemon grass
1 tsp salt
1 tsp shrimp paste

• Pound together dried chilies and salt until a fine paste is obtained. Add galangal and lemon grass, pound thoroughly.
• Add the remaining ingredients, pound well after each adding.

Mutsamun curry paste
Nam phrik kaeng mutsamun

3	large dried red spur chilies, seeded and soaked
5	roasted shallots
2	bulbs roasted garlic
1	tsp roasted sliced galangal
1	tbsp roasted sliced lemon grass
1	tbsp ground roasted coriander seeds
1	tsp ground roasted cumin
2	ground roasted cloves
1	tsp white pepper
1	tsp salt
1	tsp shrimp paste

• Pound dried chilies and salt thoroughly. Add galangal and lemon grass, and pound well.
• Add roasted garlic, roasted shallots, coriander seeds, cumin, pepper, cloves and shrimp paste. Pound well after each adding to obtain a fine paste.

Phanaeng curry paste
Nam phrik kaeng phanaeng

5	large dried red spur chilies, seeded and soaked
5	sliced shallots
10	cloves sliced garlic
1	tsp finely sliced galangal
1	tsp sliced lemon grass
$^1/_2$	tbsp finely sliced kaffir lime rind
1	tsp finely sliced coriander root
$^1/_2$	tsp white pepper
1	tsp salt
1	tsp shrimp paste

• Pound dried chilies and salt together well. Add galangal, lemon grass, kaffir lime rind and coriander root, continue pounding until mixed well.
• Add shallots and garlic, follow with pepper and shrimp paste. Pound well after each adding.

Phrik khing curry paste
Nam phrik phat phrik khing

3   large red spur chilies,
    seeded and soaked
7   sliced shallots
2   bulbs garlic
1   tbsp sliced lemon grass
1   tsp sliced coriander root
1   tsp finely sliced kaffir lime rind
1   tsp salt
5   peppercorns
2   tsp ground dried shrimp
1   tsp shrimp paste

• Pound dried chilies, salt and peppercorns together well. Add galangal, lemon grass, kaffir lime rind and coriander root. Pound together finely.

• Add garlic and shallots. Follow with dried shrimp and shrimp paste, pound well after each adding until a smooth paste is obtained.

Roasted chili paste
Nam phrik phao

5   large dried red spur chilies, roasted
8   roasted shallots
6   cloves roasted garlic
1   cup ground dried shrimp
$^1/_4$ tsp salt
3   tbsp fish sauce
1   tbsp palm sugar
$1^1/_2$ tbsp tamarind juice
2   cups vegetable oil

• Pound roasted chilies and salt together well. Follow with roasted shallots and garlic, continue pounding until mixed well.

• Add shrimp paste, pound lightly to combine. Transfer the mixture to a pan, sauté in oil until fragrant. Season to taste with fish sauce, sugar and tamarind juice, stirring well.

pork satay

[moo sateh]

500	grams pork loin
1/2	cup coconut cream
1	tsp finely chopped galangal
1	tbsp finely chopped lemon grass
1	tsp finely sliced turmeric
2	tsp ground roasted coriander seed
1/2	tsp ground roasted cumin seed
1/4	tsp ground pepper
1	tsp salt, 2 tsp sugar
	bamboo skewers
	fresh cabbage for garnish

satay sauce

1/4	cup red curry paste (see p. 21)
2	cups coconut milk
1/2	cup coarsely ground roast peanut
1/4	cup sugar, 1 1/2 tsp salt
1/4	cup tamarind juice

cucumber relish

1	red spur chili, finely sliced
4	cucumbers
2	shallots, finely sliced
1	tbsp chopped coriander
1/4	tsp salt
2	tbsp sugar
1 1/3	cups vinegar

▸▸Mix the roasted peanut with the curry paste. Heat 1 cup of coconut milk over medium heat until oil surfaces, add the curry paste mixture and stir well. Add the remaining coconut milk, stir again, then reduce the heat. Stir constantly to prevent from sticking. Season to taste with sugar, tamarind juice and salt. When the sauce thickens, remove and leave to cool. Stir lightly and turn out onto a sauce dish.

▸▸Wash the cucumbers, cut into quarters lengthwise, then cut across into thin slices. Mix vinegar, sugar and salt together, simmer over medium heat until dissolved and the sauce slightly thickens. Remove from the heat and allow to cool. Just before serving, pour the cold sauce over the vegetables, and sprinkle chopped coriander on top.

▸▸Wash the pork, cut into thin slices about 1" wide and 3" long. Pound galangal, lemon grass and turmeric finely. Toss with the pork. Add the remaining ingredients, toss well and leave to marinate for 30 minutes.

▸▸Thread the meat lengthwise and char-grill over medium heat until done. Brush occasionally with the marinade.

▸▸Arrange on a serving dish, serve with satay sauce and cucumber relish.

Serves 6

step-by-step

1. Wash the pork, cut into thin slices about 1" wide and 3" long.

2. Pound galangal, lemon grass and turmeric together well.

3. Toss the galangal mixture with the pork. Add salt, pepper, sugar, coconut cream, coriander seeds and cumin seeds. Toss well and leave to marinate for 30 minutes.

4. Char-grill over medium heat, brush occasionally with the marinade until the pork is done.

deep-fried spring rolls
[paw pia thawt]

500	grams spring roll sheet
100	grams mung bean noodle
200	grams minced pork or chicken
100	grams crabmeat
1	egg
1/2	cup shredded cabbage
1/2	cup shredded carrot
1/3	cup dried ear mushroom, soaked until tender and finely sliced
1	tbsp chopped garlic
1/2	tbsp ground black pepper
1	tbsp light soy sauce
4	cups cooking oil, for deep-frying spring onion tips, sprig of sweet basil for garnish

chili sauce

1/2	tbsp crushed red spur chili
2	tbsp water mix with 1 tbsp of tapioca flour
1	tsp salt
1/2	cup sugar
1/4	cup vinegar
1/4	cup water

▶▶ Mix vinegar, water, sugar, salt and chilies together, simmer over medium heat until hot. Stir in the tapioca batter, cooking until the sauce thickens, turn off the heat.

▶▶ Soak the noodles for 15 minutes or until soft, drain and cut into short lengths. Mix the pork or chicken, crabmeat, egg, cabbage, carrot, mushrooms, black pepper and light soy sauce together. Add 1 cup of noodle, and mix well.

▶▶ Sauté the garlic in 3 tbsp of oil until golden and fragrant, add the pork and noodle mixture. Stir until it becomes fairy dry, remove and allow to cool.

▶▶ Spread a spring roll sheet on a flat surface, place 2 tbsp of the filling in the center, fold both sides of the sheet to cover the filling and roll tightly, seal the wrapper with the thick batter. Preheat the oil over medium-low heat until hot. Deep-fry spring rolls until crispy and golden brown. Remove and drain on absorbent paper.

▶▶ Arrange on a serving dish, garnish with spring onion tips and sweet basil. Serve hot with chili sauce.

Serves 6

Tip: *The thick batter is made from 2 tbsp of wheat flour and 1/4 cup of water. Stir over low heat until the batter is done and clear, remove from the heat.*

step-by-step

1. Mix the minced pork, crabmeat, egg, cabbage, carrot, mushrooms, pepper, salt and soy sauce together. Add the mung bean noodles, toss to mix well.

2. Sauté the mixture with fried garlic over medium heat until dry, remove and put aside as the filling.

3. Fold both sides of the spring roll sheet, roll tightly and seal close with the thick batter.

4. Deep-fry the spring rolls in hot oil over medium-low heat until golden, remove and drain.

fried bread with minced pork spread

[khanom pang naa moo]

10	slices sandwich bread
1½	cups minced pork
1	beaten egg
1	coriander plant, leaves only
1	finely shredded red spur chili
1	tsp coriander root, chopped finely
1	tbsp coarsely chopped garlic
½	tsp pepper
1	tbsp light soy sauce
2	tbsp water
4	cups cooking oil, for deep-frying

▶▶Pound coriander roots, garlic and pepper finely to obtain a smooth paste, add into the minced pork. Follow with half of the beaten egg, soy sauce and water. Knead well.

▶▶Cut the bread into quarters, dry in a low temperature oven. Spread 1 tbsp of pork mixture on each piece of bread, and form a dome at the center. Brush with the remaining beaten egg, decorate with coriander leaves and red chili. Continue until finished.

▶▶Put the oil in a wok, and place over medium-low heat until hot. Deep-fry the bread spread-side down until crispy and golden brown on both sides, remove and drain on absorbent paper.

▶▶Arrange on a serving dish, enjoy while hot with cucumber relish (see p. 26).

Serves 5

step-by-step

1. Knead minced pork with other ingredients until well-combined.

2. Cut each slice of bread into quarters.

3. Spread the pork mixture on each piece of bread, and form a dome at the center.

4. Deep-fry in hot oil until golden on both sides, remove from the oil and drain.

fried bread with prawn spread

[khanom pang naa kung roi ngaa]

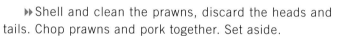

8	slices sandwich bread
300	grams prawn
100	grams pork tenderloin, diced
1	egg
1	tsp finely chopped coriander root
1	tbsp chopped garlic
2	tbsp white sesame seed
¼	tsp pepper
¼	tsp salt
2	tsp light soy sauce
3	cups cooking oil, for deep-frying

dipping sauce

¼	cup marmalade
¼	cup vinegar
¼	tsp salt

▸ Place all the ingredients for the dipping sauce in a pot, stir over low heat until the mixture thickens, remove from the heat and transfer to a sauce dish.

▸▸ Remove the crust of the bread and cut in half lengthwise. Dry the bread in a low temperature oven. This will cause the bread to absorb less oil and to be crispy.

▸ Shell and clean the prawns, discard the heads and tails. Chop prawns and pork together. Set aside.

▸▸ Pound garlic, coriander roots and pepper to obtain a fine paste. Knead the paste with the prawn mixture, break in an egg, and season with soy sauce and salt. Continue kneading until the mixture becomes uniform.

▸ Divide the prawn mixture into 16 portions, spread each portion at the centre of the bread, sprinkle sesame seeds over.

▸ Heat the oil in a wok over medium-low heat, fry the bread spread-side down until golden brown on both sides, remove and drain on absorbent paper.

▸ Arrange on a serving dish, and serve immediately with the dipping sauce.

Serves 4

step-by-step

1. Chop the prawns and pork together until they mix well.

2. Knead the minced meat with garlic paste, egg and seasonings to obtain a well-combined mixture.

3. Sprinkle white sesame seeds over the prawn topping.

4. Deep-fry in hot oil until golden on both sides, remove and drain.

rice crackers served with minced prawn sauce

[khao tang naa tang]

300 grams rice cracker or sandwich bread

$^{1}/_{2}$ cup minced pork, $^{1}/_{2}$ cup minced prawn

1$^{3}/_{4}$ cups coconut milk, $^{1}/_{4}$ cup ground roasted peanut

1 dried red spur chili, seeded and soaked in water

1 tbsp finely sliced garlic, 1 tsp finely sliced coriander root

1 tbsp finely sliced shallot, 1 chopped coriander plant

$^{1}/_{4}$ tsp pepper, 2 tbsp sugar

1-2 tbsp fish sauce

4 cups cooking oil, for deep-frying

▸▸ Preheat the oil over medium heat. Fry the rice crackers a few pieces at a time. Turn to brown on both sides, remove and drain.

▸▸ Pound the garlic, coriander root, dried chili and pepper finely.

▸▸ Bring the coconut milk to the boil over medium heat. When a film of oil surfaces, add the coriander paste and sauté until fragrant. Add minced prawns and pork, stir to combine and cooked through.

▸▸ Season to taste with sugar and fish sauce, stir well. When the mixture returns to the boil, stir in peanut and shallots. Remove from the heat, sprinkle fresh coriander over the top. Serve with fried rice crackers or toast.

Serves 3-4

step-by-step

1. Fry the rice crackers, few pieces at a time, in hot oil over medium heat until golden on both sides.

2. Pound garlic, coriander roots, pepper and dried chili to get a fine paste.

3. Sauté the paste in coconut milk until fragrant, add pork and prawns. Stir well and cook until done.

4. When the mixture starts boiling, add roasted peanuts and shallots and stir to combine.

crab croquette
[poo jaa]

- 3 crabs, 1 cup minced pork, 2 eggs
- 1 coriander plant, leaves only
- 1 finely shredded red spur chili
- $^1/_2$ tbsp crushed coriander root
- 1 tsp crushed garlic, $^1/_4$ tsp pepper
- $^1/_4$ tsp salt, 3 tbsp breadcrumb
- $1^1/_2$ tbsp light soy sauce, 3 cups cooking oil

▸▸ Clean the crab thoroughly, steam until done. Remove all the meat. Wash the shells, pat-dry and reserve for the croquette.

▸▸ Mix the crabmeat, pork, coriander roots, garlic, pepper, soy sauce and salt with 1 egg. Fill the mixture into the crab shells or small bowls. Steam over boiling water on high heat for 10 minutes or until done. Remove from the steamer and leave to cool. Remove the crab cakes from the dishes (This is not necessary if the mixture is filled in the crab shells).

▸▸ Heat the oil over medium heat until hot. Beat the remaining egg well, dip the crab cakes in the beaten egg, and coat with breadcrumbs. Deep-fry in hot oil until golden brown and cooked through. Remove from the oil and drain (If the crab shells are used, brush the egg and coat the breadcrumbs only on the surface, and fry spread-side down).

▸▸ Arrange on a serving dish, sprinkle coriander leaves and shredded chili over. Best when served hot with chili sauce.

Serves 6

step-by-step

1. Knead the crabmeat with minced pork, coriander roots, garlic, all the seasonings and an egg.

2. Steam the crab mixture over hot boiling water on high heat for 10 minutes until cooked through. Leave to cool before removing from the bowls.

3. Dip the crab cakes in the beaten egg, coat with breadcrumbs, then deep-fry in hot oil until golden and done.

4. Remove from the oil and drain.

curried fish cakes
[thawt man plaa]

500	grams spinach mackerel, minced or chopped finely
1	tbsp red curry paste (see p. 21)
1	egg
1/2	cup yard-long bean, finely sliced
3	tbsp kaffir lime leaf, finely shredded
1	tsp salt
1	tsp sugar
3	cups cooking oil, for deep-frying
	slices of pineapple
	and spring onion tips (about 3" long) for garnish

▸ Place all ingredients in a large mixing bowl, and mix well by hand. Knead and toss the mixture against the bowl until it becomes stiff.

▸ Shape the mixture into small patties about 2" in diameter, using 2 tbsp of mixture per patty. Deep-fry in hot oil over medium heat until golden brown. Remove from the oil and drain, continue shaping and frying until the mixture is used up.

▸ Arrange on a serving dish, garnish with pineapple slices and spring onion tips. Serve with cucumber relish (see p. 26)

Serves 5

step-by-step

1. Mix all the ingredients together by hand, knead and toss it against the bowl until stiff.

2. Shape the mixture into small patties about 2" in diameter.

3. Deep-fry in hot oil over medium heat until golden and done.

4. Remove from the oil and drain. Continue frying until finished.

fried pork balls

[moo paan kawn thawt]

2 cups minced pork (both lean meat and fat)
1 tbsp garlic, well pounded
2 tsp coriander root, well pounded
$^1/_2$ tsp pepper
$^1/_2$ tsp salt
1 tbsp fish sauce
2 tbsp water
3 cups cooking oil, for deep-frying
    fresh vegetables: tomato, pineapple
    spring onion tips for garnish

‣ Mix minced pork, salt, fish sauce, pepper, garlic, coriander roots and water together.

‣ Form a small ball from 1 tbsp of pork mixture, continue rolling until the mixture is used up.

‣ Put the oil in a wok, and place over medium heat. When the oil is hot, fry the pork balls until lightly brown and cooked through, remove and drain.

‣ Arrange on a serving dish, and serve with pineapple slices and tomatoes. Garnish with spring onion tips as a finishing touch.

Serves 4

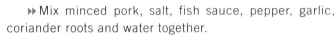

step-by-step

1. Mix all the ingredients together.

2. Roll the mixture into small balls.

3. Deep-fry pork balls in hot oil over medium heat until golden and done.

4. Remove from the oil and drain.

stuffed chicken wings
[peek kai sawt sai thawt]

```
   6  chicken wings
1 1/2  cups minced pork, 2  eggs
 1/2  cup mung bean noodle, soaked until soft, drained
       and cut into 1/2" strips (made from 50 grams dry noodle)
 1/2  cup thinly sliced water chestnut
   1  tbsp chopped coriander, 1  tbsp finely chopped garlic
 1/3  cup wheat flour, 1  tsp salt
   1  cup breadcrumb, 1  tbsp light soy sauce
   3  cups cooking oil, for deep-frying
       sweet basil sprigs for garnish
```

▸▸ Wash the chicken wings, de-bone carefully and use a sharp pointed knife to cut from the end while using your fingers to pull down the meat.

▸▸ To make the stuffing: Mix the pork, mung bean noodles, coriander, water chestnuts, garlic, salt, soy sauce, 1 egg, and 2 tbsp wheat flour together. Stuff the mixture into the boneless chicken wings, not too full. Continue until finished, arrange on a plate.

▸▸ Steam the stuffed chicken wings over boiling water on medium heat for 15 minutes until cooked through, remove and allow to cool on a rack.

▸▸ Place a wok of oil over medium heat until hot. Toss the chicken wings in the remaining flour, dip in the beaten egg and coat with breadcrumbs. Deep-fry until golden brown. Remove from the oil and drain.

▸▸ Arrange on a serving dish, garnish with sweet basil and serve with chili sauce.

Serves 6

step-by-step

1. Mix the mung bean noodles, coriander, water chestnuts, egg, garlic, wheat flour, minced pork, salt and soy sauce together.

2. Stuff into the chicken wings, not too full.

3. Steam the stuffed chicken wings over boiling water on medium heat for 15 minutes until cooked through.

4. Deep-fry in hot oil over medium heat until golden. Remove and drain.

sweet corn patties

[thawt man khao phoht]

2	cups sweet corn kernel
1	egg
2	tsp finely crushed garlic
2	tsp wheat flour
$1/2$	tsp pepper
1	tsp salt
3	cups cooking oil, for deep-frying

▸ Mix all ingredients together well.

▸ Put the oil in a wok, and place over medium heat. Shape the corn mixture into small patties, about 1-1$1/2$" in diameter, dip into the hot oil and fry until golden and cooked through. Continue shaping and frying until finished. Remove the patties from the oil and drain on absorbent paper.

▸ Arrange on a serving dish, serve immediately with chili sauce or tomato ketchup.

Serves 4

step-by-step

1. Mix all the ingredients together well.

2. Shape the corn mixture into small patties about 1-1$1/2$" in diameter, and fry.

3. Deep-fry in hot oil until golden and done.

4. Remove from the oil and drain. Continue frying until finished.

hot and sour prawn soup
[tom yum kung]

6	giant fresh water prawns, about 100 grams each
200	grams straw mushroom, halved
5-6	hot chilies, lightly crushed
5	slices matured galangal
2	stems lemon grass, cut diagonally
2-3	kaffir lime leaves, torn
2	coriander plants, cut into short length
3	tbsp fish sauce
¼	cup lime juice
3	cups chicken stock

▸▸Wash, shell and de-vein the prawns, remove the heads but keep the tails intact.

▸▸Bring a pot of chicken stock to the boil. Add lemon grass, galangal and cook for a few minutes until fragrant. Then add the prawns; follow with mushrooms and boil until cooked through (about 5 minutes).

▸▸Season with lime juice, chilies and fish sauce. Sprinkle kaffir lime leaves and coriander, turn off the heat. Transfer to a serving bowl and serve piping hot.

Serves 4

step-by-step

1. Wash, shell and de-vein the prawns. Remove the heads but keep the tails intact.

2. Cut the lemon grass diagonally into slices.

3. Bring a pot of chicken stock to the boil, add the lemon grass and boil until fragrant. Add the prawns.

4. Add kaffir lime leaves and coriander into the seasoned soup.

chicken galangal in coconut cream soup
[tom khaa kai]

500	grams chicken breast
3¹/₂	cups coconut milk
7-8	slices fresh young galangal
300	grams angel mushroom, torn into pieces
9	crushed hot chilies
1	lemon grass, cut into 1" length
4-6	kaffir lime leaves, torn in half
2	tbsp sliced coriander
3	tsp sugar
2-3	tbsp fish sauce
¹/₃	cup lime juice
1	cup water
	kaffir lime leaves for garnish

▶▶Wash the chicken, remove the skin and cut diagonally into bite-sized pieces, set aside.

▶▶Put the coconut milk in a pot, add water and bring to the boil over medium heat. When it starts to boil, reduce the heat. Add galangal, lemon grass and kaffir lime leaves, continue boiling for a few minutes until there is fragrant smell.

▶▶Add the chicken and all the seasonings, simmer until the chicken is done and tender. Add mushrooms, and cook until done. Follow with crushed chilies, then remove from the heat.

▶▶To serve: Spoon the soup into a serving bowl, stir lightly to combine and garnish with kaffir lime leaves.

Serves 4

step-by-step

1. Cut the chicken breast diagonally into bite-sized pieces.

2. Cook the galangal, lemon grass and kaffir lime leaves in the coconut milk until fragrant.

3. Add the chicken, and season to taste with sugar, fish sauce and lime juice.

4. Simmer until the chicken is tender. Add mushrooms, continue cooking until done. Then add hot chilies.

hot and sour chicken soup
[tom yum kai]

400 grams chicken breast
100 grams straw mushroom, halved
  6 cherry tomatoes, halved
 10 hot chilies, crushed lightly
  3 stems lemon grass, cut diagonally
  5 kaffir lime leaves, torn
 $^1/_2$ tsp sugar
  3 tbsp fish sauce
  4 tbsp lime juice
  3 cups chicken stock

▶▶ Wash the chicken breast, cut diagonally into pieces about $^1/_2$ cm thick, 2 cm wide and 4 cm long.

▶▶ Pour the chicken stock into a pot, and bring to the boil over medium heat. Add lemon grass and kaffir lime leaves, cook until boiling. Add the chicken and mushrooms and continue cooking until everything is cooked through.

▶▶ Season to taste with fish sauce, sugar and lime juice. When it starts boiling, add tomatoes and chilies, bring back to the boil then turn off the heat. Spoon onto a serving dish and serve hot.

Serves 4

step-by-step

1. Cut the chicken breast diagonally into slices about $^1/_2$ cm thick, 2 cm wide and 4 cm long.

2. Add lemon grass and kaffir lime leaves into a pot of boiling chicken stock over medium heat.

3. When it returns to boil, add chicken.

4. Season with fish sauce, lime juice and sugar, then add tomatoes.

mung bean noodle soup
[kaeng jeut wunsen]

1	cup mung bean noodle, soaked and cut into short length (from 100 grams dry noodle)
1	cup minced pork
6	prawns, shelled
100	grams ear mushroom or champignon mushroom, sliced
1	tbsp spring onion, cut into short length
1	tsp coriander root, finely sliced
5	cloves garlic
$1/4$	tsp pepper
3	tbsp fish sauce or light soy sauce, if preferred
3	cups pork stock
2	tbsp cooking oil
	spring onion tips for garnish

▶▶Pound the coriander roots, garlic and pepper finely.

▶▶Sauté the garlic mixture in hot oil over medium heat until fragrant. Add the pork and prawns, fry until done.

▶▶Season with 1 tbsp fish sauce. Add $1/2$ cup of the stock, follow with mung bean noodles and mushrooms.

▶▶Continue frying for 5 minutes, then transfer everything to a pot. Add the remaining $2^1/_2$ cups stock, and bring to the boil. Season to taste with fish sauce, then remove from the heat. Garnish with spring onion and serve hot.

Serves 4

step-by-step

1. Pound coriander roots, garlic and pepper finely to be a paste (use a mortar and a pestel).

2. Sauté the garlic paste over medium heat until fragrant, add pork and prawns.

3. Season with 1 tbsp fish sauce, add $1/2$ cup pork stock. Follow with mung bean noodles and ear mushrooms.

4. Transfer to a pot, add pork stock and bring to the boil over medium heat. Season to taste with fish sauce.

mung bean noodle spicy salad

[yum wunsen]

100 grams mung bean noodle
  1/2 cup boiled or steamed pork,
      thinly sliced
  1/2 cup boiled pig liver, thinly sliced
  1/2 cup boiled or steamed prawn,
      thinly sliced
  1/4 cup dried shrimp, crisp-fried
  1/2 cup spring onion,
      cut into short length
  1/2 cup celery, cut into short length
      sliced red chili, lettuce and sprig
      of celery for garnish

dressing

  1 red spur chili, finely sliced
  1 tsp pickled garlic, finely sliced
      crosswise
  1 tbsp coriander root, thinly sliced
  1 tsp salt
  1/4 cup vinegar
  1/4 cup sugar

▶ To make the dressing: Pound the coriander roots, pickled garlic and chili coarsely, transfer to a pot. Add vinegar, sugar and salt and bring to the boil over low heat. Remove from the heat, and allow to cool.

▶ Soak the mung bean noodles in water for 15 minutes or until soft, drain and cut into short strips about 3-4" long. Blanch 2 cups of soaked mung bean noodle in boiling water for 2 minutes until done and clear, drain and transfer to a mixing bowl. Toss well with the spicy dressing.

▶ Add pork, liver, and prawns to the mixture and toss to combine. Follow with spring onion and celery, and toss lightly.

▶ Arrange the mixture on a bed of lettuce on a serving dish, and sprinkle with fried dried shrimps. Garnish with celery sprigs and red chili as a finishing touch.

Serves 4

step-by-step

1. Mix vinegar, sugar and salt in a pot of pounded chili mixture, simmer over low heat until boiling.

2. Soak the mung bean noodles for 15-20 minutes or until soft. Then drain and cut into short strips about 3-4" long.

3. Pour the spicy dressing over the cooked mung bean noodles.

4. Add spring onion and celery, and toss well with the mung bean noodles and mixed meat.

winged bean spicy salad
[yum thua poo]

300	grams winged bean
$^{1}/_{2}$	cup boiled pork, sliced into small pieces
$^{1}/_{2}$	cup coconut milk
2	tbsp shallot, finely sliced and crisp-fried
2	tbsp ground roasted peanut
1	tsp chili powder
2	tbsp roasted sliced shallot
1	tbsp roasted sliced garlic
5-7	fried dried hot chilies
1	tbsp sugar
2	tbsp fish sauce
2	tbsp lime juice
	fresh iceberg lettuce and red cabbage for garnish

▸▸ Blanch the winged beans in boiling water for 3 minutes until done, transfer immediately to soak in cold water. Once cool, drain and slice into small pieces.

▸▸ Place a pot of coconut milk over low heat until boiling, remove from heat and divide into 2 portions.

▸▸ Finely pound chili powder, roasted shallots and garlic. Add sugar, fish sauce and lime juice, mix thoroughly. Transfer to a mixing bowl.

▸▸ Add winged beans, pork, 1 part of coconut milk, fried shallots and peanuts, toss well. Arrange on a bed of fresh vegetables, spoon the remaining coconut milk over the salad and serve with fried dried chilies.

Serves 4

step-by-step

1. Blanch the winged beans in boiling water for 3 minutes until done. Remove and soak immediately in cold water.

2. Cut the cooked beans into small slices.

3. Pour the spicy dressing into a mixing bowl.

4. Toss well with winged beans, pork, 1 part of coconut cream, fried shallots and roasted peanuts.

muslim-style salad
[salad khaek]

1 potato
3 hard-boiled eggs, cut into wedges
1 piece firm white beancurd
1 lettuce
1 cup bean sprout, blanched
5 cucumbers, sliced crosswise
1 onion, sliced into rings
2 tomatoes, sliced crosswise
3 cups cooking oil

dressing

2 dried spur chilies,
  seeded and soaked in water
2 cups coconut milk
2 boiled egg yolk
1/4 cup shallot, finely sliced
1/2 cup ground roasted peanut
1 tsp curry powder
1/4 tsp salt
1/3 cup sugar
3 tbsp fish sauce
1/4 cup tamarind juice

▸▸ To make the dressing: Pound chilies, salt, shallots and curry powder finely, transfer to a mixing bowl. Add peanuts and egg yolks, stirring together. Simmer 1 cup of coconut milk over low heat until oil surfaces. Add the curry paste and sauté until fragrant. Pour in the remaining coconut milk, season with fish sauce, sugar and tamarind juice. Turn off the heat.

▸▸ Peel and thinly slice potatoes crosswise, soak in water to prevent discoloration, and drain well. Fry in hot oil over medium heat until crisp and golden. Cut the beancurd into thin slices, fry until crisp, drain and set aside.

▸▸ Arrange all ingredients nicely on a serving dish, spoon the dressing over the mixture just before serving, toss lightly and serve at once.

Serves 6

step-by-step

1. Pound dried chilies, salt, shallots and curry powder to obtain a smooth paste.

2. Simmer 1 cup of coconut milk over low heat until oil surfaces. Add the curry paste and sauté until fragrant.

3. Add the remaining coconut milk, season with fish sauce, sugar and tamarind juice. Turn off the heat.

4. Fry potato in hot oil over medium heat until golden and crispy.

pork, chicken and prawn spicy salad

[yum saam sahai]

1¹/₂ cups steamed or boiled pork, thinly sliced
1¹/₂ cups steamed or boiled chicken, thinly sliced
1¹/₂ cups steamed or boiled prawn, thinly sliced
¹/₄ cup roasted peanut or cashew nut, broken into chunks
shredded cabbage and carrot, lettuce for garnish

dressing

3 tbsp roasted chili paste (see p. 24)
1 tsp sugar
3 tbsp fish sauce
¹/₄ cup lime juice
2-3 tbsp tamarind juice

▸▸ Make the spicy dressing by mixing roasted chili paste, fish sauce, sugar and tamarind juice in a pot. Simmer the mixture over low heat until boiling. Remove from heat and allow to cool slightly, add lime juice and stir to mix well.

▸▸ Transfer the dressing to a mixing bowl, add the pork, chicken, and prawns and toss thoroughly. Spoon the mixture onto a bed of lettuce, shredded cabbage and carrot on a serving dish and sprinkle peanuts or cashew nuts on top just before serving.

Serves 6

step-by-step

1. Simmer the spicy dressing over low heat until boiling.

2. Add lime juice into the warm dressing, stir well and leave to cool.

3. Toss the pork, prawns and chicken with the spicy dressing.

4. Sprinkle the nuts over the top before serving.

piquant prawn salad
[plah kung]

500	grams giant fresh water prawn
5	sliced hot chilies
2	stems sliced lemon grass
3	sliced shallots
1/2	cup mint leaf
2	shredded kaffir lime leaves
1	tbsp lime juice
1	tbsp fish sauce
	cabbage for garnish

▸▸Clean the prawns, shell and de-vein. Remove the heads and tails. Blanch in boiling water until just done, remove and cut in half lengthwise.

▸▸Mix the prawns with lime juice, fish sauce, lemon grass, chilies, shallots and kaffir lime leaves, toss to mix well.

▸▸Spoon onto a bed of fresh cabbage and sprinkle mint leaves over and serve.

Serves 4

step-by-step

1. Wash the prawns, shell and de-vein. Discard the heads and tails.

2. Blanch the prawns in boiling water until just done.

3. Transfer the cooked prawns into a mixing bowl, add lime juice, fish sauce, lemon grass, hot chilies, shallots and kaffir lime leaves.

4. Toss all the ingredients well.

squid spicy salad
[yum plaa muek]

300	grams fresh squid
3	tbsp spring onion, cut into short length
1/4	cup thinly sliced shallot
1/4	cup finely shredded young ginger
1/4	cup finely sliced lemon grass
1/4	cup mint leaf
	Chinese cabbage, green and red hot chilies for garnish

dressing

3	hot chilies
2	tbsp finely sliced garlic
1/4	cup lime juice
3-4	tbsp fish sauce

▶▶ To make the dressing: Pound the chilies and garlic coarsely, add lime juice and fish sauce, and stir well.

▶▶ Wash the squid, discard bones, skin and eyes and wash again. Make a crisscross pattern on the flesh and cut into pieces about 2"x2". Blanch in boiling water until done, remove and transfer to a mixing bowl.

▶▶ Gently toss with shallots, lemon grass, ginger, spring onion and the spicy dressing.

▶▶ Spoon onto a bed of Chinese cabbage leaves on a serving dish, sprinkle mint leaves over and garnish with chilies as a finishing touch.

Serves 4

step-by-step

1. With a knife, make a crisscross pattern on the squid.

2. Cut the squid into 2"x2" pieces.

3. Blanch the squid in hot boiling water until done, remove and transfer to a mixing bowl.

4. Spoon the spicy dressing over the squid and other ingredients, gently toss.

boiled egg spicy salad
[yum khai tom]

5	boiled eggs
$1/4$	cup finely sliced shallot
$1/4$	cup finely shredded green mango or green apple
$1/4$	cup mint leaf
2	tbsp spring onion, cut into short length about $1/2$" long
	lettuce, shredded cabbage and carrot,
	sprig of mint leaf for garnish

dressing

4	chopped hot chilies
2	tbsp pickled garlic, finely sliced crosswise
3	tbsp lime juice
1	tsp salt

▸▸ Make the spicy dressing by mixing all ingredients together, put aside.

▸▸ Shell the boiled eggs, slice crosswise into rings about $1/4$" thick. Arrange on a bed of lettuce, shredded cabbage and shredded carrot on a serving dish.

▸▸ Put sliced shallots, green mango, mint leaves and spring onion in a mixing bowl. Pour the spicy dressing over and toss lightly to mix well. Spoon over the boiled eggs, garnish with mint leaves and serve immediately.

Serves 2

step-by-step

1. Mix lime juice, pickled garlic, salt and hot chili together to make the spicy dressing.

2. Use the egg slicer to slice the egg into rings about $1/4$" thick. Arrange on a bed of lettuce, shredded cabbage and shredded carrot.

3. Pour the spicy dressing into a mixing bowl, add shallots, mango, mint leaves and spring onion, and toss lightly.

4. Spoon the mango dressing over the boiled eggs, garnish with mint leaves. Toss lightly before eating.

grilled chicken spicy salad
[yum kai yaang]

2	pieces grilled chicken breast
3	spring onions, cut into pieces about 1¹/₂" long
	lettuce leaves, Chinese cabbage, spring onion tips
	(cut into pieces 3"-4" long) and tomato slices for garnish

dressing

1	tsp minced red spur chili
1¹/₂	tbsp ground roasted peanut
¹/₄	tsp salt
1	tsp sugar
2	tbsp fish sauce
2	tbsp vinegar
2	tbsp lime juice

▸▸ To make the dressing: Add all ingredients except peanuts to a pot, and bring to the boil over medium heat. Turn off the heat, add peanuts and stir well.

▸▸ Cut the chicken into slices and put in a mixing bowl. Toss well with the spicy dressing. Follow with spring onion and toss again.

▸▸ Arrange on a bed of lettuce and Chinese cabbage on a serving dish, garnish with spring onion tips and tomato slices, serve at once.

Serves 4

1. Bring the spicy dressing to the boil over medium heat.

2. Add roasted peanuts into the dressing, stir well.

3. Slice the grilled chicken into pieces.

4. Add spring onion into the spicy grilled chicken, toss lightly to combine.

sausage and ham spicy salad

[yum saikrawk kap ham]

150	grams Frankfurter sausage
150	grams cooked ham slices
100	grams roasted cashew nut
1	onion, sliced crosswise
	Chinese cabbage, carved carrot and spring onion tips (about 2-3" long) for garnish

dressing

2	tbsp roasted chili paste
$^1/_2$	tsp salt
1	tbsp lime juice
3	tbsp tamarind juice

▸▸ Put roasted chili paste, tamarind juice and salt in a pot, stir well. Simmer over low heat until boiling. Add lime juice, remove from the heat and allow to cool slightly, stir well.

▸▸ Slice the sausages diagonally about $^1/_4$" thick. Cut the ham into squares about $^1/_2$x$^1/_2$".

▸▸ Combine onion, sausages and ham in a mixing bowl, pour over the dressing and toss well. Add cashew nuts and toss lightly. Transfer onto a bed of Chinese cabbage leaves, add a personal touch with carved carrot and spring onion tips as a garnish.

Serves 4

step-by-step

1. Simmer the spicy dressing over low heat until boiling, add lime juice. Remove from the heat and stir well.

2. Slice the sausages diagonally about $^1/_4$" thick.

3. Toss the spicy dressing with onion, sausages and ham thoroughly.

4. Add cashew nuts and toss again.

canned sardine spicy salad
[yum plaa krapawng]

2	cans sardine in tomato sauce
2	tbsp finely shredded young ginger
1/4	cup finely sliced shallot
1	tbsp spring onion, cut into short length about 1" long
1	tbsp spring onion, finely sliced
1/4	cup mint leaf

dressing

1/2	tsp sliced hot chili
1/4	tsp salt
3	tbsp lime juice

▸▸ To make the dressing: Thoroughly mix together hot chili, salt and lime juice.

▸▸ Toss the sardines with young ginger and shallots. Add the spring onion and mint leaves, and toss again lightly.

▸▸ Transfer to a serving dish, scatter sliced spring onion on top before serving.

Serves 2

step-by-step

1. Stir hot chili, salt and lime juice together.

2. Toss the sardines thoroughly with ginger and shallots.

3. Add the spicy dressing and toss well.

4. Add spring onion and mint leaves, toss lightly to combine.

spicy chopped pork
[laap moo]

2	cups minced pork tenderloin
100	grams boiled or steamed pig liver, sliced
1	tbsp chopped coriander
2	tbsp spring onion, cut into short length
$^1/_2$	cup mint leaf
2	tbsp shallot, sliced thinly
$^1/_2$	tsp chili powder
2	tbsp ground roasted rice or breadcrumb
6	tbsp lime juice
2	tbsp fish sauce
4	crisp-fried dried hot chilies
	fresh vegetables: cabbage, Chinese cabbage, cucumber, yard-long beans, coriander leaves and spring onion

▸▸Add 4 tbsp of lime juice into minced pork, toss well then squeeze out liquid. Cook the liquid over medium heat until boiling, add the pork and cook until done, then turn off the heat. Transfer to a mixing bowl, mix with cooked liver and shallots (reserve some for garnish). Toss well to combine.

▸▸Season to taste with fish sauce and lime juice. Add chili powder and roasted rice, toss again. Sprinkle the spring onion, coriander and mint leaves, toss lightly.

▸▸Arrange on a bed of Chinese cabbage leaves on a serving dish, scatter the remaining sliced shallots and fried dried chilies on top. Serve with fresh vegetables.

Serves 4

step-by-step

1. Mix the minced pork with lime juice, squeeze and reserve the liquid.

2. Heat the liquid until boiling, add minced pork and sauté until cooked through.

3. Add shallots into a mixing bowl, toss well with cooked minced pork and liver.

4. Season to taste with fish sauce and lime juice. Toss again with chilli powder and ground roasted rice.

spicy chopped chicken
[laap kai]

3	cups chicken breast or tenderloin, coarsely chopped
3	spring onions, cut into short length
2	tbsp coriander, coarsely chopped
¹/₄	cup mint leaf
5	shallots, thinly sliced
¹/₂	tsp chili powder
2	tbsp ground roasted rice or breadcrumb
1	tsp salt
¹/₄	cup lime juice
1	tbsp fish sauce
	fresh vegetables: cabbage,Chinese cabbage, cucumber, yard-long beans and spring onion

▸▸ Put the chicken and salt in a wok, fry over medium heat until the meat turns white and done. Turn off the heat, transfer to a mixing bowl. Add shallots (reserve some for garnish),and toss well.

▸▸ Season to taste with lime juice and fish sauce. Sprinkle chili powder and ground roasted rice over the mixture and mix well. Add spring onion, coriander and mint leaves, toss lightly.

▸▸ Arrange on a serving dish, sprinkle the remaining sliced shallots on top. Serve with fresh vegetables.

Serves 6

1. Fry the chicken with salt over medium heat until done.

2. Toss the cooked chicken with sliced shallots thoroughly.

3. Season with lime juice and fish sauce. Toss again with chili powder and roasted rice.

4. Add spring onion, chopped coriander and mint leaves and toss lightly to combine.

spicy grilled beef
[neua naam tok]

500 grams beef top round,
  1 tbsp spring onion, cut into short length
 $^1/_4$ cup coriander, chopped
  1 tbsp lemon grass, thinly sliced
 $^1/_4$ cup shallot, thinly sliced
 $^1/_4$ cup mint leaf
 $^1/_2$ tsp chili powder
 $^1/_4$ tsp sugar
 $1^1/_2$ tbsp ground roasted rice or breadcrumb
 $4^1/_2$ tbsp lime juice
  3 tbsp fish sauce
    fresh vegetable: Chinese cabbage, cabbage,
    red cabbage and spring onion

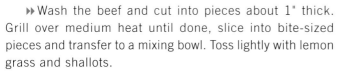

▸▸Wash the beef and cut into pieces about 1" thick. Grill over medium heat until done, slice into bite-sized pieces and transfer to a mixing bowl. Toss lightly with lemon grass and shallots.

▸▸Season to taste with fish sauce, lime juice and sugar. Add chili powder and ground roasted rice, toss well to combine. Add mint leaves, spring onion and coriander, toss again.

▸▸Arrange on a serving dish and serve.
Serves 6

1. Slice the grilled beef into bite-sized pieces.

2. Toss the grilled beef with lemon grass and shallots in a mixing bowl.

3. Season with fish sauce, sugar and lime juice. Toss again with chili powder and ground rice.

4. Add mint leaves, spring onion and coriander and toss lightly.

spicy roast pork
[plah moo op]

500	grams pork tenderloin
4	stems thinly sliced lemon grass
5	shallots, finely sliced
3	kaffir lime leaves, finely shredded
$^1/_2$	cup mint leaf
3	tbsp spring onion, cut into short length
3	tbsp coriander, chopped
5	crisp-fried dried hot chilies
1	tsp ground black pepper
1	tbsp seasoning sauce, 1 tbsp whisky
	lettuce for garnish

dressing

10	hot chilies, 15 cloves garlic, $^1/_2$ tsp salt
1	tsp sugar, 1 tbsp fish sauce, 4 tbsp lime juice

▸▸ Pound chilies, garlic and salt together, spoon into a bowl, season with lime juice, fish sauce and sugar, stir until sugar has dissolved.

▸▸ Wash the pork, marinate with seasoning sauce, whisky, and black pepper for 15 minutes. Place in an oven-proof dish, and roast in an oven at 450°F for 15-20 minutes or until done, slice into pieces about $^1/_2$ cm thick.

▸▸ Thoroughly toss the cooked pork with lemon grass, shallots, kaffir lime leaves, spring onion and the spicy dressing. Transfer onto a bed of lettuce on a serving dish, sprinkle fried dried chilies on top and serve immediately.

Serves 4

step-by-step

1. Mix the lime juice, fish sauce and sugar into the pounded chili mixture. Stir until the sugar has all dissolved.

2. Toss the pork with seasoning sauce, whisky and black pepper. Marinate for 15 minutes.

3. Slice the roast pork into pieces about $^1/_2$ cm thick.

4. Add the spicy dressing into a mixing bowl, and toss well with roast pork and the remaining ingredients.

piquant minced pork salad
[naem sot]

    1   cup minced pork
  $1/2$ cup finely sliced boiled pig skin
  $1/4$ cup finely shredded young ginger
  $1/4$ cup finely sliced shallot
    1   tbsp finely sliced garlic
  $1/4$ cup finely chopped coriander and spring onion
  $1/2$ cup roasted peanut
    5   fried dried hot chilies
    1   tsp salt
  3-4 tbsp lime juice
       fresh vegetables: spring onion, cabbage, Chinese cabbage

▸▸Sprinkle $1/2$ tsp of salt over the pork and dry-fry over low heat until done, breaking the meat into small pieces. Turn off the heat, and allow to cool, then add pig skin, and mix thoroughly. Season with salt, lime juice, ginger, garlic and shallots. Toss well to combine.

▸▸Spoon onto a serving dish. Sprinkle roasted peanuts, spring onion, coriander and fried chilies. Enjoy with fresh vegetables.

Serves 2

step-by-step

1. Dry-fry minced pork with salt over low heat, break into small pieces and fry until done.

2. Transfer to a mixing bowl and leave to cool. Add boiled pig skin and stir well.

3. Season with salt and lime juice. Follow with ginger, garlic and shallots.

4. Toss together well.

green papaya salad
[som tam malakaw]

1	cup green papaya, peeled and shredded
1/4	cup ground dried shrimp
1	dried chili, soaked in water and drain
7	peppercorns
6	cloves garlic
1/4	cup finely shredded lime rind
3	tbsp palm sugar
3	tbsp fish sauce
1	tbsp lime juice
1	tbsp tamarind juice
	fresh vegetables: Chinese cabbage, cabbage, yard-long beans, Thai convolvulus, etc.
	red and green hot chilies for garnish

▸▸Pound the papaya lightly in a mortar, remove and set aside.

▸▸Pound the garlic, dried chili and peppercorns thoroughly, transfer to a mixing bowl.

▸▸Mix tamarind juice, fish sauce and sugar together, and bring to the boil over medium heat. Remove from the heat, and allow to cool. Add lime juice, pour into the chili mixture, stir well. Put aside as the dressing.

▸▸Add papaya, dried shrimp and lime rind in the mixing bowl and toss well. Arrange on a bed of Chinese cabbage, garnish with red and green hot chilies and serve with fresh vegetables.

Serves 2

step-by-step

1. Pound the shredded papaya lightly, put aside.

2. Put in the pounded garlic and chili into a mixing bowl.

3. Pour the cold sauce to mix with the chili mixture, stir well.

4. Add papaya, dried shrimp and lime rind. Toss well to combine.

green beef curry
[kaeng khiaw waan neua]

400	grams beef
3	tbsp green curry paste (see p. 21)
2¹/₂	cups coconut milk
	(squeezed out from 400 grams grated coconut)
5	small eggplants, quartered
2-3	red spur chilies, sliced diagonally
2	kaffir lime leaves, torn
¹/₄	cup sweet basil leaf
1¹/₂	tbsp fish sauce
1¹/₂	tsp palm sugar
1	tbsp cooking oil
	sweet basil leaves and red chili slices for garnish

▶▶ Slice the beef into thin pieces, about 3 cm thick.

▶▶ Sauté the curry paste in oil over medium heat until fragrant, reduce the heat, gradually add 1¹/₂ cups of the coconut milk a little at a time, stir until a film of green oil surfaces.

▶▶ Add the beef and kaffir lime leaves, continue cooking for 3 minutes until fragrant and the beef is cooked through. Transfer to a pot, place over medium heat and cook until boiling. Add the remaining coconut milk, season with sugar and fish sauce. When the mixture returns to the boil add the eggplants. Cook until the eggplants are done, sprinkle sweet basil leaves and red chilies over, then turn off the heat.

▶▶ Arrange on a serving dish and garnish with sweet basil leaves and red chilies before serving.

Serves 4

step-by-step

1. Slice the beef into thin strips, about 3 cm thick.

2. Gradually add coconut milk a little at a time, stir until the oil surfaces and 1¹/₂ cups of the coconut milk is used up.

3. Add the beef and kaffir lime leaves, continue cooking for further 3 minutes until the beef is done.

4. When it returns to boil, add eggplants and cook until done. Then add red chili and sweet basil leaves.

beef in phanaeng curry
[phanaeng neua]

400	grams beef
3	tbsp *phanaeng* curry paste or red curry paste (see p. 23)
2	cups coconut milk
6	kaffir lime leaves, torn
1/4	cup ground roasted peanut
1/4	tsp salt
3	tbsp palm sugar
2 1/2	tbsp fish sauce
	slices of red chili for garnish

▸▸ Wash the beef, cut into pieces about 3 cm thick.

▸▸ Heat 1 cup of coconut milk over medium heat until the oil surfaces. Add curry paste, stir constantly for 2 minutes until fragrant and red oil surfaces. Add the beef, and cook for a further 5 minutes or until done. Add the remaining coconut milk.

▸▸ Season to taste with salt, fish sauce and sugar. Add roasted peanuts, stir well. Reduce the heat and simmer for 15 minutes or until the beef is tender. Stir well to combine. Sprinkle kaffir lime leaves on top, and turn off the heat.

▸▸ Transfer to a serving dish, garnish with red chilies. Serve hot.

Serves 4

step-by-step

1. Heat 1 cup of coconut milk over medium heat until a film of oil surfaces.

2. Sauté the curry paste for 2 minutes until fragrant and red oil surfaces.

3. Add the beef and fry for further 5 minutes until the beef is done.

4. Pour in the remaining coconut milk. Add roasted peanuts after seasoning with salt, fish sauce and sugar. Stir well to combine.

mutsamun chicken curry
[kaeng mutsamun kai]

500	grams chicken thigh
3	tbsp mutsamun curry paste (see p. 23)
1	cup coconut cream,
2	cups coconut milk
5	potatoes, carved and boiled
5	small onions, carved
2	tbsp roasted peanut
5	roasted cardamom pods
1	roasted cinnamon stick, about 1" long
3	bay leaves, 3 tbsp palm sugar
2	tbsp fish sauce, 3 tbsp tamarind juice
3	tbsp lemon juice
	bay leaves for garnish

▸▸ Preheat the coconut milk over medium heat until boiling, add chicken thigh, reduce the heat and simmer for 15 minutes until tender.

▸▸ Preheat the coconut cream over medium heat until oil surfaces. Add the curry paste, and sauté until fragrant. Transfer to the chicken pot, add peanuts. Season to taste with sugar, fish sauce, tamarind juice and lime juice.

▸▸ Add the remaining ingredients, and simmer until everything is tender and cooked through.

▸▸ Spoon onto a serving dish, garnish with bay leaf to give a sense of a Thai touch. Pickled ginger or cucumber relish (see p. 26) can also be served as condiments.

Serves 4

step-by-step

1. Cook the chicken thigh in the coconut milk over low heat for 15 minutes until tender.

2. Sauté the curry paste until fragrant, transfer to the chicken pot.

3. Add roasted peanuts, season with sugar, fish sauce, tamarind juice and lime juice.

4. Add onion, potatoes, bay leaves, cardamom and cinnamon. Simmer until everything is tender and cooked through.

prawn indian yellow curry
[kaeng kari kung]

800	grams tiger prawn
1	tbsp yellow curry paste (see p. 22)
2¹/₂	cups coconut milk
8	cherry tomatoes, quartered
2	red spur chilies, sliced diagonally
¹/₂	tsp salt
1¹/₂	tsp palm sugar
1	tbsp fish sauce

▸▸Wash, shell and de-vein the prawns, remove the heads but keep the tails intact.

▸▸Pour 1 cup of coconut milk into a wok and place over medium heat. Heat until boiling and the oil lightly surfaces. Add the curry paste, stir until fragrant.

▸▸Season to taste with fish sauce, sugar and salt. Add the remaining coconut milk and continue cooking for 5 minutes.

▸▸Add tomatoes, prawns and chilies. When mixture returns to the boil, turn off the heat. Serve with cucumber relish. (see p. 26)

Serves 4

step-by-step

1. Shell the prawns, remove the heads but keep the tails intact, and de-vein.

2. Season to taste with fish sauce, sugar and salt.

3. Add the remaining coconut milk and continue cooking for a few minutes.

4. Add tomatoes and prawns, follow with red spur chilies.

red curry with roast duck
[kaeng phet pet yaang]

1	roast duck
1/4	cup red curry paste (see p. 21)
4	cups coconut milk
1	cup miniature eggplant
10	cherry tomatoes
4	kaffir lime leaves, torn
1	tsp palm sugar
1/2	tsp salt
2	tbsp fish sauce
1/2	cup water or chicken stock
1 1/2	tbsp cooking oil
	kaffir lime leaves for garnish

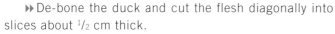

▶ De-bone the duck and cut the flesh diagonally into slices about 1/2 cm thick.

▶ Fry the curry paste in oil over medium heat until fragrant. Add 1 cup of coconut milk, stir thoroughly until red oil surfaces.

▶ Add the duck meat and sauté for 1 minute. Transfer the mixture to a pot, add the remaining coconut milk and chicken stock and stir well. Add the tomatoes, eggplants and kaffir lime leaves.

▶ Season to taste with sugar, salt and fish sauce. Continue cooking until the mixture returns to the boil, then turn off the heat.

▶ Spoon onto a serving dish, garnish with kaffir lime leaves and serve hot.

Serves 6

step-by-step

1. Slice the roast duck into thick pieces about 1/2 cm thick.

2. Add roast duck and fry for 1 minute.

3. Transfer to a pot, add the remaining coconut milk, chicken stock, eggplants and tomatoes. Follow with kaffir lime leaves.

4. Season to taste with fish sauce, sugar and salt. Cook until boiling.

chicken and bamboo shoot in red curry

[kaeng phet kai sai nawmai]

400	grams boneless chicken breast
300	grams bamboo shoot, sliced thinly
3	tbsp red curry paste (see p. 21)
2	cups coconut milk
2	red spur chilies, sliced diagonally
$^1/_2$	cup sweet basil leaf
5	kaffir lime leaves, torn
2	tbsp fish sauce
$^1/_4$	tsp salt
$1^1/_2$	tsp palm sugar
	sweet basil leaves for garnish

▸▸Wash the chicken, slice diagonally into $^1/_2$ cm thick, 3 cm wide and 3 cm long pieces.

▸▸Thinly slice the bamboo shoots.

▸▸Pour 1 cup of the coconut milk into a wok. Bring to the boil over medium heat, stir constantly. Add the curry paste, stir until red oil surfaces. Add the chicken and sauté until it turns white and done.

▸▸Add the remaining coconut milk, follow with the bamboo shoots. Season with fish sauce, sugar and salt and bring back to the boil.

▸▸Sprinkle kaffir lime leaves, chilies and sweet basil leaves, then turn off the heat. Arrange on a serving dish and garnish with sweet basil leaves before serving.

Serves 5

step-by-step

1. Cut the bamboo shoots into thin slices.

2. Bring the coconut milk to the boil over medium heat, add the curry paste and sauté until red oil surfaces.

3. Add the chicken and cook until done.

4. Add kaffir lime leaves, red spur chilies and sweet basil leaves before turning off the heat.

stuffed chicken wings in phanaeng curry

[phanaeng peek kai sawt sai]

10	chicken wings
3	tbsp *phanaeng* curry paste (see p. 23)
3	cups coconut milk
1	cup finely minced chicken breast
2	red spur chilies, sliced diagonally
1/2	cup sweet basil leaf
2	tbsp kaffir lime leaf, shredded finely
2	tbsp palm sugar, 3 tbsp fish sauce
	toothpicks
	sprig of sweet basil for garnish

▶▶ Wash the chicken wings, de-bone carefully, using a sharp pointed knife to cut from the end while using your fingers to pull down the meat.

▶▶ Add 1 tbsp each of curry paste and fish sauce into minced chicken, mix well. Stuff into the chicken wings—not too full, and secure with toothpicks.

▶▶ Arrange on a dish and steam over boiling water on high heat for 15 minutes or until done. Turn off the heat, move from the steamer and leave to cool. Remove the toothpicks.

▶▶ Heat 1 cup of coconut milk over medium heat until a film of oil surfaces. Stir in the curry paste, gradually add the remaining coconut milk a little at a time while stirring, cook until red oil surfaces. Season to taste with fish sauce and sugar. Add the stuffed chicken wings, and cook for a few minutes. Transfer to a pot, close the lid and simmer over low heat until the wings are tender and most of the liquid has evaporated. Turn off the heat.

▶▶ Transfer to a serving plate, garnish with kaffir lime leaves, chilies, and basil leaves.

Serves 5

step-by-step

1. Use a sharp pointed knife gently de-bone the chicken wings.

2. Use your fingers to pull down the meat while continue de-boning to the middle part, then remove the bone.

3. Stuff the mixture into the chicken wing—not too full, and secure with toothpicks.

4. Season with fish sauce and sugar before adding the chicken wings, stir lightly to combine.

chicken and wax gourd curry
[kaeng khua fak]

500	grams wax gourd
500	grams chicken breast
3	tbsp *kaeng khua* curry paste (see p. 22) or red curry paste
1	cup coconut cream
2	cups coconut milk
1	red spur chili, sliced diagonally
5	kaffir lime leaves, torn
3	tbsp palm sugar
3	tbsp fish sauce
1	tbsp tamarind juice

▸▸Clean the chicken, remove skin and cut diagonally into bite-sized pieces. Peel the gourd, discard the seeds and cut into 1" chunks.

▸▸Heat the coconut cream over medium heat until the oil surfaces. Fry the curry paste until fragrant and red oil surfaces. Add the chicken, continue cooking for a few minutes until the chicken is white and done.

▸▸Transfer to a pot, add the remaining coconut milk and stir well. Add in the gourd. Cook over medium heat until the gourd is done, season to taste with sugar, fish sauce and tamarind juice.

▸▸When the curry boils again, sprinkle kaffir lime leaves and red chili over it and turn off the heat.

Serves 4

step-by-step

1. Cut the chicken diagonally into pieces.

2. Cut the wax gourd into slices about 1" thick.

3. Sauté the curry paste in coconut cream until fragrant and red oil surfaces. Add chicken and fry until cooked through.

4. Add the wax gourd into the curry, simmer over medium heat until done.

chu chee curry with mackerel
[chuu chee plaa thoo sot]

400	grams fresh mackerel or other meaty fish
2	tbsp red curry paste (see p. 21)
3	cups coconut milk
3	red spur chilies, sliced diagonally
2	kaffir lime leaves, finely shredded
1/2	cup sweet basil leaf
2	tbsp palm sugar
3	tbsp fish sauce
	sprig of sweet basil and carved red chili for garnish

▸ Scale and clean the fish, remove the head and the insides. Wash again, score diagonally on both sides.

▸ Heat 1 cup of coconut milk over medium heat until the oil surfaces, add the curry paste, stir constantly for 2 minutes until fragrant. Gradually add the remaining coconut milk. When the mixture starts boiling, add the fish and cook until done, do not stir.

▸ Season to taste with fish sauce and sugar, stir lightly to combine. Then turn off the heat.

▸ Transfer to a serving dish, garnish with shredded kaffir lime leaves, red chilies and sweet basil leaves as a finishing touch.

Serves 4

step-by-step

1. Scale lightly on both sides of the fishes.

2. Stir in the curry paste, sauté until fragrant.

3. Gradually add the remaining coconut milk.

4. When it comes to the boil, add the fish and cook until done. Do not stir.

southern-style braised chicken
[kai kaw lae]

4 pieces chicken thigh,
about 150 grams each

5 cups coconut milk

2 tbsp palm sugar

3 tbsp fish sauce

3 tbsp lime juice

$^1/_2$ cup butter

3 cups cooking oil

red hot chilies for garnish

curry paste

5 dried red spur chilies, seeded and
soaked in water

2 tbsp shallot, sliced thinly

1 tbsp chopped garlic

1 tsp finely sliced fresh turmeric or
curry powder

$^1/_4$ tsp ground roasted coriander seed

$^1/_4$ tsp ground roasted cinnamon

$^1/_4$ tsp ground roasted nutmeg

1 tsp salt

1 tsp shrimp paste

replacement for curry paste

mix 1 tsp of turmeric powder or
curry powder with 3 tbsp of
red curry paste (see p. 21)

▶ Pound the chilies and salt thoroughly, add garlic and shallots, turmeric (or curry powder), coriander seeds, cinnamon, nutmeg, and pound well. Follow with shrimp paste, pound to mix well.

▶ Clean the chicken, and drain. Fry in butter and oil over medium heat until golden and cooked, transfer to a pot. Add the coconut milk, and place over medium heat. When the coconut milk starts to boil, reduce the heat and simmer for 30 minutes or until the chicken is tender.

▶ In the same wok, drain away the oil and leave only $^1/_2$ cup. Sauté the curry paste over medium heat until fragrant. Transfer to the chicken pot, season with fish sauce, lime juice and sugar. Simmer until the chicken is tender and absorb most of the sauce.

▶ Arrange on a serving dish. Garnish with red chilies as a finishing touch before serving.

Serves 4

step-by-step

1. Pound the curry paste finely.

2. Fry the chicken in butter and oil over medium heat until golden and done.

3. Transfer the fried chicken to a pot, add the coconut milk and place over medium heat.

4. Add the sautéed curry paste into the chicken pot.

steamed fish curry
[haw mok]

400 grams fish, chicken or pork
2 cups coconut milk
1 egg
1 shredded red spur chili
¼ cup coriander leaf
2 cups sweet basil leaf
3 tbsp shredded kaffir lime leaf
2 tsp rice flour
3 tbsp fish sauce

curry paste

5 dried red spur chili,
seeded and soaked in water
3 bulbs garlic
2 tbsp galangal, sliced finely
2 tbsp lemon grass, sliced finely
1 tsp kaffir lime rind, sliced finely
1 tbsp shredded wild ginger *(krachai)*
2 tsp finely sliced coriander root
5 peppercorns
½ tsp salt
1 tsp shrimp paste

▸▸ Pound the ingredients for the curry paste well to obtain a smooth paste, set aside.

▸▸ Cut the fish into thin slices; if the chicken is used, cut into small pieces, if the pork is used, chop coarsely.

▸▸ Pour ½ cup of the coconut milk into a pot, add rice flour and stir until dissolved. Simmer over low heat until done, remove from the heat, and set aside as the topping.

▸▸ Add the curry paste to 1 cup of coconut milk in a mixing bowl, add the fish and stir well. Break in an egg and season with fish sauce. Add the remaining coconut milk a little at a time while stirring until all the coconut milk is used up. Stir for further 20 minutes, then add ½ cup of basil leaf, 2 tbsp coriander, and 1 tbsp kaffir lime leaf. Stir well.

▸▸ Line the cups with the basil leaves, fill each cup full with the mixture, and steam over boiling water on high heat for 15 minutes. Remove the steamer from the heat, top each cup with a spoon of the prepared coconut cream, scatter coriander, kaffir lime leaves, and chili on top, then return to the heat. Continue steaming for 1 minute, remove from the steamer.

Serves 6

step-by-step

1. Stir 1 cup of coconut milk with the curry paste, add the fish and stir well.

2. Gradually add the coconut milk and keep on stirring until all the coconut milk is used up.

3. Line the banana containers with sweet basil leaves, spoon the mixture into the containers until full.

4. Sprinkle coriander leaves, kaffir lime leaves and red chili over the top. Continue steaming for 1 minute, remove from the steamer.

thai-style vegetable soup
[kaeng liang]

```
400  grams tiger prawn
  1  cup pumpkin, cut into slices
  1  cup bottle gourd, peeled and cut into slices
  1  cup baby corn, cut into slices
  1  cup straw mushroom, halved
  1  cup loofah, peeled and cut into slices
  1  cup hairy basil leaf, 2-3  tbsp fish sauce
  4  cups chicken stock
     hairy basil sprigs for garnish
```

spicy paste

```
 10  peppercorns, 1/2  cup ground dried shrimp or dried fish
  1  tbsp shrimp paste, 10  shallots, thinly sliced
```

▸▸ Wash, shell and de-vein the prawns, remove the heads and tails. Cut in half lengthwise and put aside.

▸▸ To prepare spicy paste: Pound peppercorns finely, follow with dried shrimps, shallots and shrimp paste. Pound well to obtain a smooth paste (use a mortar and pestel).

▸▸ Bring the chicken stock to the boil over medium heat, add the spicy paste and stir well. When the mixture starts boiling again, add the pumpkin. Once the pumpkin is cooked, add the bottle gourd, baby corn and loofah. Continue cooking until everything is done.

▸▸ Add the prawns, season with fish sauce. When it returns to the boil, sprinkle the hairy basil leaves and turn off the heat. Transfer to a serving dish, garnish with hairy basil sprigs and serve hot.

Serves 4

step-by-step

1. Pound all ingredients for the spicy paste finely to obtain a smooth paste.

2. Shell and de-vein the prawns, remove the heads and tails and cut into half lengthwise.

3. Add the spicy paste into a pot of boiling chicken stock over medium heat and stir well.

4. When the soup comes to the boil, add the vegetables.

barbecued spareribs
[see khrong moo yaang]

1	kilogram pork sparerib
1½	tbsp finely chopped mature ginger
1	tsp pepper
¼	tsp ground cinnamon
¼	tsp ground nutmeg
1	tsp salt
3	tbsp light soy sauce
3	tbsp whisky
	slices of lemon, lemon rind and iceberg lettuce for garnish

▸ Cut the spareribs into pieces about 5" long.

▸ Toss the ribs with soy sauce and whisky. Add the remaining ingredients and put aside to marinate for 1 hour.

▸ Char-broil the ribs over low heat until done and golden brown.

▸ Cut into 2" pieces, arrange on a serving dish with iceberg lettuce, lemon slices and shredded lemon rind. Serve hot.

Serves 8

step-by-step

1. Cut the spareribs into pieces about 5" long

2. Toss the ribs with soy sauce and whisky.

3. Add salt, ground nutmeg, ground cinnamon, ginger and pepper. Toss well and marinate for 1 hour.

4. Cut the grilled ribs into pieces about 2" long.

grilled pork
[moo yaang]

1 kilogram pork shoulder, cut into 2"x4"x4" pieces
2 tsp juice from pounded fresh mature ginger
1 tsp salt
4 tbsp sugar
2 tbsp honey
2 tbsp sherry
2 tbsp light soy sauce
1 tbsp sesame oil
   fresh vegetables: cucumber, tomato
   coriander leaves and spring onions for garnish

▶ Marinate the pork with other ingredients for at least 6 hours.

▶ Grill the pork until done, brushing occasionally with the marinade while grilling.

▶ Slice the grilled pork and arrange on a serving dish. Garnish with coriander leaves and green shallots as a finishing touch.

▶ Serve with sweet chili sauce (see p. 28) and fresh vegetables.

Serves 6

step-by-step

1. Marinate the pork with all ingredients for 6 hours.

2. Brush the marinade on the pork while grilling.

3. Grill until the pork is cooked through.

4. Cut the pork at an angle into slices.

pork stew
[moo tom khem]

1	kilogram pork tenderloin, cut into cubes
6	hard-boiled eggs, shelled
1	tbsp chopped coriander root
1	tbsp chopped garlic
1	tbsp peppercorn
1	tsp salt
1½	tbsp palm sugar
3	tbsp fish sauce
¼	cup dark soy sauce
1	tbsp brandy
2	cups chicken stock
2	cups water
1	tbsp cooking oil
	coriander leaves for garnish

▸▸Combine all ingredients except pork and eggs with 1 cup of water. Marinate the pork in this mixture for 20 minutes.

▸▸Heat the oil in a wok over high heat, add the pork and the marinade, stir to mix well. Transfer to a pot, add water and bring to the boil over medium heat. Add boiled eggs, and simmer for 30 minutes until the pork is tender. Spoon onto a serving bowl and sprinkle coriander leaves on top.

Serves 6

step-by-step

1. Mix 1 cup of water with all ingredients, stir lightly to combine. Add the pork and toss well.

2. Fry the pork and the marinade in a wok.

3. Transfer to a pot, add the remaining water.

4. When it becomes boiling, add boiled eggs and simmer for 30 minutes.

sweet and sour spareribs
[seekhrong moo phat priaw waan]

- 1 kilogram pork sparerib,
  cut into 2" length
- 1/4 cup chili, sliced diagonally
- 1/2 cup pineapple, cut into cubes
- 1/2 cup onion ring
- 1/4 cup tomato, cut into wedges
- 2 tbsp corn flour
- 1 tsp pepper
- 1 tsp salt
- 1 tsp Chinese wine
- 1 tbsp light soy sauce
- 1/4 cup vegetable oil, for stir-frying
- 4 cups vegetable oil, for deep-frying

sweet&sour sauce

- 1/2 cup tomato ketchup
- 1/4 cup shredded young ginger
- 1 tsp pepper
- 1 tsp salt
- 1 tbsp sugar
- 1 tbsp vinegar
- 3 cups soup stock

▶▶ Toss the ribs with 1 tbsp of corn flour, pepper, salt, Chinese wine and soy sauce. Leave to marinate for 2-3 hours, then fry in hot oil over medium heat until golden brown. Remove and drain, arrange on a serving dish.

▶▶ Mix the ingredients for the sauce in a pot, and bring to the boil over medium heat. Once boiling, reduce the heat and simmer for 15 minutes. Turn off the heat and set aside.

▶▶ Place a wok of oil over medium heat. When the oil is hot, sauté the chilies, pineapple, tomatoes and onion, stir well. Add 1 cup of the sauce, and stir to combine. Mix the remaining corn flour with 3 tbsp water, add into the wok and stir until the sauce thickens and is clear. Turn off the heat. Spoon over the fried spareribs.

Serves 6

step-by-step

1. Toss the ribs well with corn flour, pepper, salt, Chinese wine and soy sauce.

2. Fry the marinated ribs in hot oil over medium heat until golden, remove and drain.

3. Simmer the ingredients for the sweet and sour sauce over low heat for 15 minutes.

4. Sauté chili, pineapple, tomato and onion until cooked through. Add 1 cup of the sauce, stir well.

sweet and sour pork
[moo phat priaw waan]

400 grams pork tenderloin, cut into bite-sized pieces
 ¹/₂ cup tomato, cut into wedges
 ¹/₂ cup cucumber, sliced diagonally
 ¹/₄ cup sliced onion
100 grams straw mushroom, halved
 1 cup spring onion, cut into 1" length
 2 spur chilies, sliced diagonally
 1 tsp chopped garlic, 1 tbsp tapioca flour
 ¹/₄ tbsp pepper, ¹/₄ tsp salt
 2 tbsp sugar, 1 tbsp fish sauce
 1 tbsp vinegar, 2 tbsp tomato sauce
 ¹/₂ cup chicken stock, 1 tbsp cooking oil

▶▶ Sauté garlic in oil over medium heat until fragrant. Add the pork and sauté until it turns white. Add mushrooms, cucumber, onion and tomato, cook until the vegetables are tender. Then add chilies and spring onion, stir well.

▶▶ Season with tomato sauce, vinegar, sugar, salt and fish sauce. Follow with half of the chicken stock, stir well to combine.

▶▶ Mix the remaining stock with tapioca flour, pour into a wok and stir until the sauce thickens and is clear. Turn off the heat.

▶▶ Transfer to a serving dish, sprinkle pepper over the top. Serve hot.

Serves 4

step-by-step

1. Fry the pork with chopped garlic until cooked through.

2. Add mushrooms, cucumber and onion. Follow with tomato, sauté until all the vegetables are tender and done.

3. Season and add half of the chicken stock.

4. Mix the remaining stock with tapioca flour and stir into the wok.

spicy stir-fried pork and yard-long beans
[phat phrik khing moo]

300	grams pork tenderloin
$^1/_4$	cup *phrik khing* chili paste (see p. 24)
200	grams yard-long bean
1	red spur chili, finely shredded
3	kaffir lime leaves, finely shredded
1	tbsp palm sugar
1	tbsp fish sauce
2	tbsp cooking oil

▸▸ Wash the pork, cut into small pieces, and toss with 1 tsp of fish sauce. Leave to marinate for 5 minutes.

▸▸ Wash the beans, blanch in hot boiling water until just cooked. Transfer to soak in cold water, drain and cut into length about 1" long or tie loosely and cut into pieces.

▸▸ Heat the oil over medium heat until hot, sauté the chili paste until fragrant. Add the pork and cook until it is done.

▸▸ Season to taste with sugar, 1 tbsp fish sauce, then add the beans. Stir well to combine. Arrange on a serving dish, sprinkle shredded kaffir lime leaves and red chili for garnish.

Serves 4

(see p. 24)

step-by-step

1. Toss the pork with 1 tsp fish sauce and leave to marinate for 5 minutes.

2. Tie the cooked beans loosely and cut into pieces, or cut into 1" long.

3. Fry the curry paste in oil over medium heat until fragrant, add the pork and stir-fry until done.

4. Season with sugar and fish sauce. Add cooked beans, stir to mix well.

spicy stir-fried pork
[phat phet moo]

400	grams pork loin, sliced thinly
1	tbsp red curry paste (see p. 21)
1	cup coconut milk
2	red spur chilies, sliced diagonally
3	sprigs green peppercorn
3-5	kaffir lime leaves, torn
$1/4$	tsp salt
$1/2$	tbsp sugar
$1^{1}/_{2}$	tbsp fish sauce
1	tbsp cooking oil

▸▸ Fry the curry paste in oil over medium heat until fragrant, add pork and fry for 5 minutes until done. Add half of the coconut milk, and stir occasionally for another 10 minutes until the oil surfaces.

▸▸ Pour in the remaining coconut milk and stir well. Season to taste with fish sauce, salt and sugar. Add kaffir lime leaves and green peppercorns, stir to mix well. When the mixture starts to boil, add red chilies and stir again.

▸▸ Transfer to a serving dish. Best served with steamed rice.

Serves 4

step-by-step

1. Fry the chili paste in oil over medium heat until fragrant.

2. Add the pork and cook for 5 minutes. Then add half of the coconut milk, stir-fry for 10 minutes until the red oil surfaces.

3. Pour in the remaining coconut milk, stir together and season to taste with fish sauce, salt and sugar.

4. Add kaffir lime leaves and green peppercorns, stir to mix well. Then add red chili and stir again.

braised pork leg with spices

[khaa moo tom pha-loh]

1	pork back leg, about 800 grams
10	cloves garlic
3	coriander roots
$^1/_2$	tsp five spices powder
20	peppercorns
1	tsp dark soy sauce
2	tbsp light soy sauce
2	cups water

sauce

2	sliced yellow chilies
1	tsp chopped coriander root
3	tbsp chopped garlic
$^1/_2$	tsp salt
2	tbsp vinegar

▶ Pound chilies, coriander roots, garlic and salt together (using a mortar and a pestel). Stir in vinegar, set aside for the sauce.

▶ Put all ingredients in a pressure cooker and add 2 cups of water. Cover and cook for 20 minutes over medium heat. Remove from the heat, and leave to cool for at least 10 minutes before opening. Discard the bone, slice the meat into pieces and arrange on a serving dish with some of the gravy. Garnish with chopped coriander, and serve with the sauce.

Serves 4

step-by-step

1. Add vinegar into the chili mixture, stir well and set aside for the sauce.

2. Put all ingredients into a pressure cooker.

3. Add 2 cups of water.

4. Cook for 20 minutes over medium heat, then remove from the heat.

braised beef soup
[neua tun]

500	grams beef shank
1	celery, cut into length about 1" long
2	lettuce plants, 300 grams bean sprout
1	tbsp coarsely chopped fresh coriander
1	piece galangal, about 1/2" length
1	crushed coriander root
1	stick cinnamon, about 1" long
2	tbsp fried garlic
1	bay leaf *(bai krawan)*
1/2	tsp pepper, 1/2 tsp salt
1/2	tsp ground black pepper
2	tbsp light soy sauce
1	tbsp dark soy sauce
10	cups water

▸▸Wash the beef, cut into 1" cubes.

▸▸Put all the spices and seasonings into a pot. Follow with beef and water. Bring to a boil over medium heat, then reduce the heat. Cover and simmer for 50 minutes until the beef is tender.

▸▸Blanch the bean sprouts and arrange in a serving dish together with sliced fresh lettuce. Spoon the braised beef and the soup over. Sprinkle chopped coriander, celery, fried garlic and pepper on top. Serve hot with steamed rice or cooked noodles.

Serves 4

Note: *If an ordinary pot is used, it will take about 50 minutes. Whereas the pressure cooker will require only 25 minutes and only 2 cups of water is needed at the beginning. When it completes 25 minutes, remove from the heat and allow to cool, open and add 3 more cups of boiled water, season to taste and bring back to the boil once again before serving.*

step-by-step

1. Cut the beef into 1" cubes.

2. Simmer the beef for 50 minutes until tender.

3. Blanch all vegetables, cut into short lengths and arrange into a serving bowl.

4. Spoon the beef soup into the bowl, sprinkle coriander, celery, fried garlic and pepper over.

stir-fried beef with oyster sauce

[phat neua naam man hawy]

400	grams beef tenderloin, cut into thin slices
200	grams straw mushroom, halved
3	shiitake mushrooms, soaked and cut into pieces
2	spring onion, cut into short length
1	red spur chili, sliced diagonally
1	tbsp chopped garlic
1	tbsp wheat flour
$^1/_2$	tsp pepper, 1 tsp sugar
2	tbsp light soy sauce
4	tbsp oyster sauce
3	tbsp cooking oil
	spring onion tips for garnish

▸▸ Marinate the beef in a mixture of the flour and light soy sauce for 15 minutes.

▸▸ Place oil in a pan, add garlic and fry over medium heat until golden and fragrant, add both kinds of mushroom and stir-fry. Follow with the beef and stir-fry until done.

▸▸ Season to taste with oyster sauce, sugar and pepper, stir well. Add spring onion and chili, stir again to combine, then remove from the heat.

▸▸ Arrange on a serving dish. Garnish with spring onion tips and serve.

Serves 3-4

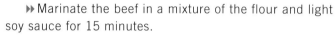

step-by-step

1. Toss the beef with wheat flour and soy sauce, leave to marinate for 15 minutes.

2. Fry chopped garlic, sauté with shiitake and straw mushrooms until done.

3. Add the marinated beef and continue cooking until the beef is done.

4. Season with oyster sauce, sugar and pepper. Then add spring onion and red chili, stir well.

fried sun-dried beef
[neua daet diaw]

400	grams beef
3	finely chopped coriander roots
1	bulb chopped garlic
$1/2$	tsp pepper
1	tbsp sugar
1	tsp curry powder
1	tbsp fish sauce
2	tbsp whisky
1	tbsp oyster sauce
3	cups cooking oil, for deep-frying
	tomato slices, cabbage and coriander for garnish

▶Clean the beef, pat-dry, cut into slices about 1 cm thick, 8 cm long. Pound the garlic, coriander roots and pepper finely, toss thoroughly with the beef. Season with fish sauce, oyster sauce and the remaining ingredients. Mix well and leave to marinate for 1 hour.

▶Arrange the beef on a rack, leave in the strong sunshine for 4 hours. Turn occasionally until dry on both sides. Pack in a plastic bag and keep in a refrigerator.

▶To serve: Fry the sun-dried beef in hot oil until fragrant and done. Remove from the oil and drain. Arrange on a serving dish and garnish with tomato slices, cabbage and sprigs of fresh coriander.

Serves 4

step-by-step

1. Cut the beef into slices about 1 cm thick, 8 cm long.

2. Toss the beef with the garlic mixture thoroughly, add the remaining ingredients and toss again to combine.

3. Arrange the marinated beef on a rack, leave in the strong sunshine for 4 hours.

4. Deep-fry in hot oil until fragrant and done. Remove from the oil and drain.

stir-fried chicken
[phat khee mao kai]

2	cups minced chicken breast or tenderloin
5	hot chilies
15	cloves chopped garlic
4	chopped coriander roots
1/2	cup holy basil leaf
1	red spur chili, sliced diagonally
1	tsp sugar
2	tbsp fish sauce
2	tbsp oyster sauce
1/4	cup chicken stock
2	tbsp cooking oil
	crisp-fried holy basil leaves for garnish

▸▸ Pound the chili, garlic and coriander roots well to obtain a smooth paste.

▸▸ Put the oil in a wok and place over medium heat until hot, fry the chili mixture until fragrant. Add the chicken, stir until done.

▸▸ Season to taste with oyster sauce, fish sauce, sugar and chicken stock. Stir thoroughly. Add holy basil leaves and spur chili, and stir again. Turn off the heat.

▸▸ Transfer to a serving dish, sprinkle fried basil leaves on top, and serve at once.

Serves 4

step-by-step

1. Pound or blend chili, coriander roots and garlic together well.

2. Sauté the chili mixture in hot oil over medium heat until fragrant.

3. Add minced chicken and cook until done. Season with sugar, fish sauce, and oyster sauce. Pour in the chicken stock.

4. Add holy basil leaves and red chili, stir to combine. Then turn off the heat.

stir-fried chicken with cashew nuts

[kai phat met mamuang himmapaan]

300 grams chicken breast, sliced thinly
$^1/_2$ cup fried cashew nut
$^1/_4$ cup crisp-fried dried spur chili, cut into 1 cm pieces
 1 red spur chili, sliced diagonally
 1 small onion, sliced
$^1/_3$ cup spring onion, cut into 1" pieces
$^1/_2$ tbsp chopped garlic
$^1/_4$ tsp salt
1$^1/_2$ tbsp fish sauce
 1 tbsp dark soy sauce
 2 tbsp cooking oil
   fresh coriander for garnish

▸▸ Fry the garlic in oil over medium heat until golden and fragrant, add the chicken and cook until done.

▸▸ Add onion, cashew nuts, fried dried chilies and spring onion, stir well.

▸▸ Season to taste with fish sauce, dark soy sauce and salt, stir again. Turn off the heat.

▸▸ Spoon onto a serving dish, garnish with red chili and fresh coriander before serving.

Serves 4

step-by-step

1. Fry the chicken with garlic until it turns white and done.

2. Add onion, cashew nuts and fried dried chilies.

3. Add spring onion and stir well.

4. Season with fish sauce, dark soy sauce and salt, stir to mix together.

thai barbecued chicken
[kai yaang]

1	chicken, about 1 kilogram, cut half
2	tbsp finely chopped mature ginger
2	tbsp finely chopped lemon grass
2	tbsp finely chopped coriander root
2	tbsp pepper, 1 tsp sugar
1^1/$_2$	tbsp curry powder
2	tbsp light soy sauce
	red bell pepper slices and Chinese cabbage for garnish

sauce

1	tbsp crushed red chili
1	tsp crushed or chopped garlic
^{1}/$_2$	tsp salt
1	tbsp sugar
^{1}/$_2$	cup vinegar

▶ Mix all ingredients for the sauce in a pot. Simmer over low heat and stir occasionally until it becomes a smooth syrup, then remove from the heat.

▶ Blend ginger, lemon grass and coriander root finely, toss well with the chicken. Add soy sauce, sugar, pepper and curry powder, toss again to mix well. Leave the chicken to marinate in a refrigerator for at least 6 hours.

▶ Char-grill the chicken over low heat until done and the skin turns lightly brown. Arrange on a serving dish and serve with the sauce.

Serves 6

step-by-step

1. Simmer the sauce over low heat until it is slightly thick.

2. Blend ginger, lemon grass and coriander roots finely. Transfer to toss thoroughly with the chicken.

3. Add soy sauce, sugar, pepper and curry powder. Toss again.

4. Grill the chicken over a low charcoal fire until golden and cooked through and the skin is lightly brown.

braised chicken in tomato sauce
[kai op naam daeng]

500 grams chicken thigh
$^1/_4$ cup chopped onion
3 bay leaves
$^1/_4$ tsp pepper
1 tsp salt, 2 tbsp sugar
1 tbsp light soy sauce
3 tbsp tomato ketchup
2 tbsp chili sauce
1 tbsp seasoning sauce
1 tbsp Worcestershire sauce
1 cup water
2 cups vegetable oil
boiled vegetables: green bean, carrot

▸▸ Wash the chicken and drain.

▸▸ Toss the chicken with salt and pepper. Fry in hot oil until golden and done. Remove from the oil and drain.

▸▸ Drain away the oil and leave only $^1/_4$ cup in the wok, fry chopped onion over medium heat until fragrant. Season with tomato ketchup, seasoning sauce, soy sauce, Worcestershire sauce, chili sauce and sugar. Add bay leaves, stir well and transfer to a pot.

▸▸ Add the fried chicken, pour in water, cover and simmer over low heat until the chicken is tender and the sauce reduces. Transfer to arrange on a serving dish, and serve with boiled vegetables.

Serves 4

step-by-step

1. Wash the chicken and drain.

2. Toss the chicken with salt and pepper, fry in hot oil until golden and done. Remove and drain.

3. Fry chopped onion over medium heat until fragrant. Season with tomato ketchup, all the sauces and sugar. Add bay leaves and transfer to a pot.

4. Add fried chicken and water. Cover and simmer over low heat until the chicken is tender and the sauce reduces.

stir-fried chicken with chili paste
[phat phrik khing kai]

500	grams sliced chicken breast
1	tbsp *phrik khing* chili paste (see p. 24)
¹/₂	cup coconut milk
4	shredded kaffir lime leaves
1	tbsp sugar
2	tbsp fish sauce
3	tbsp cooking oil

▸▸Sauté the chili paste in oil over medium heat until fragrant. Add the coconut milk and stir well. Add chicken and fry until done.

▸▸Season to taste with fish sauce and sugar, stir again to combine. Spoon onto a serving dish, sprinkle kaffir lime leaves over the top and serve.

Serves 4

(see p. 24)

step-by-step

1. Sauté the chili paste in oil over medium heat until fragrant.

2. Stir in the coconut milk.

3. Add chicken and cooking until done.

4. Season to taste with fish sauce and sugar. Stir well to combine.

stir-fried chicken with water chestnuts
[kai phat haew]

500	grams chicken breast
10	canned water chestnuts
1	leek, cut into 2" length
4	slices fresh ginger
1	tbsp coarsely sliced celery
1	tbsp chopped garlic
$^1/_2$	tbsp sugar
$^1/_4$	cup light soy sauce
1	tbsp sherry
1	cup water
$^1/_4$	cup cooking oil

▸▸Clean the chicken, remove the skin and cut into bite-sized pieces.

▸▸Place a wok over medium heat, add the oil and heat until hot, sauté ginger and garlic until fragrant. Add the chicken, stir-fry until golden brown and cooked.

▸▸Season to taste with soy sauce, add sherry and water. Cover the wok and simmer over low heat.

▸▸Add water chestnuts, leek and sugar, continue cooking for 15 minutes until the chicken is tender. Spoon onto a serving dish. Best when served hot.

Serves 4

step-by-step

1. Cut the chicken breast diagonally into pieces.

2. Sauté ginger and garlic over medium heat until fragrant. Add the chicken and cook until golden and done.

3. Season to taste with soy sauce and sherry. Add in some water.

4. Add water chestnuts, leek and sugar, continue frying for 15 minutes until the chicken is tender.

steamed egg
[khai tun]

2 eggs
3 prawns
3 tbsp minced pork
1 coriander plant, leaves only
1 spring onion, chopped
1 tbsp shallot, thinly sliced
$1/4$ tsp pepper
$1/4$ tsp salt
2 tbsp light soy sauce
1 cup chicken stock

▶ Clean the prawns, shell and de-vein, remove the heads but keep the tails intact. Divide minced pork into 3 portions and wrap 1 portion around each prawn.

▶ Beat the eggs in a mixing bowl, add chicken stock, light soy sauce, pepper, and salt. Follow with shallots and spring onion, stir well. Pour the egg mixture into 3 cups, steam over boiling water on medium heat for 5 minutes.

▶ When the egg mixture begins to set, place a wrapped prawn on top of each bowl, continue steaming until cooked through; about 15 minutes. Remove from the steamer, sprinkle coriander leaves on top. Serve and enjoy while steaming hot.

Serves 2

step-by-step

1. Wrap minced pork over the prawns closely.

2. Add shallots and spring onion into the egg mixture, stir well.

3. Steam the egg mixture over boiling water on medium heat for 5 minutes.

4. When the egg custard begins to set, place the wrapped prawn on top. Steam for further 15 minutes until the pork and prawns are done.

roast stuffed duck
[pet thawd sawt sai]

1	whole duck, about 2 kilograms
2½	cups minced pork
1	egg
2	tbsp pounded mixture of garlic, coriander root and pepper
¼	cup onion, cut into small cubes
¼	cup carrot, cut into small cubes
¼	cup pea
1	tsp sugar
3	tbsp light soy sauce
2	tbsp seasoning sauce
2	tbsp butter
	slices of red bell pepper and dill sprig for garnish

gravy

¼	cup juice from the roast duck
2	tsp wheat flour
⅛	tsp pepper
¼	tsp salt

▸▸ Heat the juice from roast duck over low heat. When it is hot, add the flour and stir quickly until well-combined. Follow with salt and pepper, stir until the flour is done and the liquid becomes a smooth gravy. Remove from the heat.

▸▸ Clean the duck, remove the feathers and separate the insides; wash and dice the liver, gizzard and heart.

▸▸ Use a small sharp pointed knife to remove the bone. Start near the vent and work up toward the neck, cut away the neck, continue around it across the back of the duck. Then, follow the same procedure on the other side. Remove the bone, and turn the duck right side out. Cut and remove the leg bone, then turn the duck right side in.

▸▸ Mix the pork with garlic mixture. Add diced innards, peas, carrots and onion; and mix together well. Break in an egg, season with light soy sauce and seasoning sauce. Fill the duck with the pork mixture, and toss thoroughly.

▸▸ Place the duck in a baking pan, and bake in an oven at 350°F for 40 minutes or until cooked through. Remove, spread the butter over the skin, re-bake at 400°F for 20 minutes or until the skin is golden brown. Remove and allow to cool before cutting into ½" slices.

▸▸ Arrange the duck on a serving dish, and garnish with slices of red bell pepper and fresh dill. Pour the prepared gravy over the duck.

Serves 4

step-by-step

1. Use a small sharp pointed knife to de-bone the duck. Carefully start from the vent and work up toward the neck.

2. Cut away the neck; continue around it across the back of the duck and follow the same procedure on the other side.

3. Remove the bone and carefully turn the right side out. Cut and remove the leg bone, and turn it in.

4. Fill the duck with the pork mixture until full.

crispy roast duck

[pet op krawp]

- 1 whole duck, about 1-2 kilograms
- 2 tsp minced mature ginger, 1 tsp ground roasted cinnamon
- $^1/_2$ tsp ground roasted nutmeg, 1 tsp pepper
- 2 tbsp light soy sauce
  fresh vegetables: spring onion, cucumber,
  lettuce, celery
  fresh iceberg, lettuce and pineapple for garnish
  aluminum foil for wrapping and greaseproof paper
  for lining

▶ Clean the duck, remove all the feathers, head, and neck. Wash again and pat dry.

▶ Mix all the spices, and divide into 2 portions. Rub the first portion over the inside of the duck, sew the duck closed. Rub the remaining mixture all over the outside.

▶ Wrap the duck with aluminum foil, place in a roasting and roast in an oven at 450°F for 1 hour. Remove and allow to cool for 15 minutes before removing the foil.

▶ Transfer the duck onto a rack which has already been lined with greaseproof paper. Prick the skin with a fork. Bring back to the oven and re-bake at 350°F for 30 minutes, remove from the oven and brush with soy sauce.

▶ Re-bake at 400°F for 5 minutes or until the skin is crisp and brown.

▶ Cut the duck in half or de-bone and cut into pieces, alternatively the crispy skin can be sliced and served separately from the meat. Serve with fresh spring onions, cucumber, lettuce, celery and sweet soy sauce.

Serves 6

step-by-step

1. Wash the whole duck and pat dry.

2. Spread the spice mixture over the inside and seal close.

3. Remove the duck from the oven, leave to cool for 15 minutes, then remove the foil.

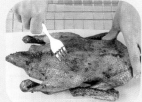

4. Place the roast duck on a rack which has already lined with greaseproof paper. Prick the skin with a fork.

fried pomfret
[plaa jalamet thawt]

1   white pomfret, about 500 grams
1   tbsp tapioca flour
3-5 finely sliced hot chilies
1-3 finely sliced shallots
1   tbsp lime juice
2   tbsp fish sauce
3   cups cooking oil
    spring onion tips, coriander leaves, sliced orange rind and
    shredded red chili for garnish

▶▶ Clean the fish well, slit down the middle and remove the insides. Score both sides nicely. Dip in the flour and shake off any excess.

▶▶ Place a wok of oil over medium heat. When the oil is hot, fry the fish until golden brown and done. Remove and drain.

▶▶ Mix the hot chilies, shallots, lime juice and fish sauce together. Set aside for the spicy sauce.

▶▶ Arrange the fried fish on a serving dish, garnish with spring onion tips, coriander leaves, orange rind and red chili. Serve hot with the spicy sauce.

Serves 2

step-by-step

1. Score both sides nicely.

2. Dip the fish in tapioca flour to coat well.

3. Fry the fish in hot oil over medium heat until golden and done.

4. Remove from the oil and drain.

fried sun-dried fish
[plaa samlee daet diaw]

1 whole black-banded trevally *(plaa samlee)*,
about 500 grams
1 tsp shredded hot chili
1 tbsp finely sliced shallot
2 tbsp shredded green sour mango
1 tsp palm sugar
2 tbsp fish sauce
3 tbsp lime juice
3 cups cooking oil
coriander leaves for garnish

▶▶ Clean the fish, butterfly, flatten and discard the bones and the insides. Wash, criscross the fish with a knife, and allow to dry for a few minutes. Then dry in strong sunshine for 5-6 hours, turn occasionally to dry on both sides.

▶▶ Place a wok over medium heat, pour in the oil and heat until hot, fry the fish until golden brown. Remove and drain, transfer to arrange on a serving plate.

▶▶ Toss the shallots, green mango and chili lightly. Season with fish sauce, lime juice and sugar. Spoon onto a sauce dish, garnish with coriander leaves and serve with the fried fish.

Serves 4

step-by-step

1. De-bone, remove the insides and butterfly the fish.

2. Drain on a rack for a few minutes, dry in the strong sunshine for 5-6 hours.

3. Deep-fry in hot oil until golden, remove and drain.

4. Making the spicy sauce by mixing shallots, green mango and chilies together. Stir in fish sauce, lime juice and sugar to taste.

steamed sea bass with lime
[plaa kraphong neung manao]

1 sea bass, about 450 grams
5 hot chilies
5 cloves peeled garlic
2 white spring onion stems cut into 1¹/₂" long pieces
3 tbsp lime juice
1¹/₂ tbsp light soy sauce
¹/₂ cup chicken stock
thin slices of lime for garnish

▶Scale the fish, slit down the middle and remove the insides. Trim off the tail end, and clean thoroughly. Score diagonally on both sides, then arrange on a plate.

▶Chop the chilies finely, mix with the stock and stir well. Follow with lime juice and light soy sauce, stir again to mix well. Pour over the fish, sprinkle spring onion and garlic on top.

▶Steam over boiling water on high heat for 10-15 minutes or until done. Remove from the steamer, garnish with slices of lime and serve while steaming hot.

Serves 4

step-by-step

1. Score the fish on both sides.

2. Mix chopped chilies with chicken stock, lime juice and soy sauce, stir well.

3. Scatter spring onion and garlic over the seasoned fish.

4. Steam over boiling water on high heat for 10-15 minutes or until done.

steamed pomfret with pickled plum

[plaa jalamet neung kiam buay]

1 white pomfret, about 500 grams
¹/₂ cup pork fat, cut into thin strips
1 finely shredded red chili
2 celery, cut into length about 1" long
1 tsp shredded young ginger
¹/₂ cup shiitake mushroom, soaked and sliced thinly
2 pickled plums
1 tsp light soy sauce

▸▸ Clean the fish thoroughly, slit down the middle and remove the insides. Score both sides, and place on a steamable dish.

▸▸ Mix the pork fat with pickled plums and soy sauce, then pour over the fish. Arrange celery and shiitake mushrooms over the fish. Follow with chili and ginger.

▸▸ Steam the fish over boiling water on high heat for 15 minutes or until done. Remove from the steamer and serve immediately.

Serves 2

step-by-step

1. Score the fish on both sides.

2. Combine pork fat, pickled plum and soy sauce together.

3. Arrange shiitake mushrooms, celery, ginger and red chili over the fish.

4. Steam over boiling water on high heat for 15 minutes until done.

steamed fish
[plaa pae-sa]

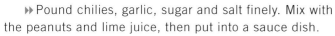

  1 whole threadfin fish, about 500 grams
$\frac{1}{4}$ cup pork fat, cut into thin strips
$\frac{1}{4}$ cup shredded young ginger
  1 celery, cut into length about 1" long
  1 red spur chili, sliced diagonally
  2 bulbs pickled garlic, finely sliced
  2 tsp sugar, 3 tbsp vinegar
  2 cups chicken stock

dipping sauce
  5 hot chilies, 1 tbsp crushed garlic
  1 tsp salt, 1 tbsp sugar, 2 tbsp lime juice
  1 tsp roasted peanut, finely ground

▶ Pound chilies, garlic, sugar and salt finely. Mix with the peanuts and lime juice, then put into a sauce dish.

▶ Scale the fish, slit down the middle and remove the insides. Wash well, score on both sides. Place it in a deep platter, arrange the pork fat over the fish. Steam over boiling water on high heat for 10 minutes or until done. Turn off the heat. Sprinkle celery, ginger, pickled garlic and red chili over.

▶ Mix the chicken stock, vinegar and sugar together, stir until dissolved. Pour the seasoned stock over the fish, and bring back to steam over boiling water on high heat for further 5 minutes. Remove and serve steaming hot with the sauce.

Serves 4

step-by-step

1. Combine pounded chili mixture with ground peanuts and lime juice to make the sauce.

2. Place the fish in a platter, arrange pork fat over the fish.

3. Sprinkle celery, ginger, pickled garlic and red chili over the steamed fish.

4. Mix the chicken stock, vinegar and sugar, and pour over the steamed fish.

baked grouper in tomato sauce

[plaa kao op sauce makheua thet]

1	grouper, about 500 grams
1	onion, sliced crosswise
1	tomato, sliced crosswise
2	bell peppers, sliced crosswise
1	tsp pepper
1	tsp sugar
1	tbsp white wine
¹/₂	cup tomato ketchup
1¹/₂	tbsp fish sauce
1	tbsp butter
	coriander leaves for garnish
	banana leaf or aluminum foil

▶ Scale the fish, chop off the head, slit down the middle, remove the insides, debone and wash thoroughly.

▶ Mix tomato ketchup, white wine, fish sauce, sugar and pepper together.

▶ Butter the banana leaf or foil, place the fish in the center of the wrapper. Pour the prepared tomato sauce over the fish, arrange the vegetables on top, then wrap tightly.

▶ Bake in an oven at 350°F for 15-20 minutes or until done. Arrange on a serving dish, garnish with coriander leaves and serve.

Serves 4

step-by-step

1. Mix the tomato ketchup, white wine, fish sauce, sugar and pepper together to make the prepared tomato sauce.

2. Butter the banana leaf or aluminum foil. Place the fish in the center of the wrapper.

3. Pour the prepared tomato sauce over the fish.

4. Arrange onion, tomato and bell peppers on top.

japanese-style grilled fish
[plaa oo yaang see-iu]

1 frigate mackerel, about 500 grams
2 tbsp finely grated Chinese radish
$^1/_4$ cup the marinade
1 tsp lemon rind, slices
fresh iceberg lettuce and lemon wedges for garnish

marinade

1 cup Japanese light soy sauce
1 cup Mirin (Japanese sweet wine)
2-3 tbsp sugar
$^1/_2$ cup finely chopped ginger

▶▶ Mix all ingredients for the marinade, reserve $^1/_4$ cup for the dipping sauce.

▶▶ Wash the fish, pat dry and fillet. Score the skin in a crisscross pattern. Toss the fish fillet in the marinade, leave to marinate for 30 minutes in a refrigerator.

▶▶ Grill the fish over medium-low heat until lightly brown and done, brush the marinade occasionally while grilling. Transfer to arrange on a serving dish, sprinkle lemon rind over and garnish with iceberg lettuce and lemon wedges. Serve with grated Chinese radish and the dipping sauce.

Serves 4

step-by-step

1. Mix all ingredients for the marinade, reserve $^1/_4$ cup for the dipping sauce.

2. Score the skin in a crisscross pattern.

3. Toss the fish with the remaining marinade.

4. Grill over medium-low heat, brush the marinade occasionally while grilling. Grill until golden and cooked through.

char-grilled prawns
[kung phao]

4	giant fresh water prawns, about 150 grams each
1¹/₂	tbsp finely chopped garlic
¹/₂	tbsp finely chopped chili
1	tsp finely chopped coriander
¹/₂	tsp salt
1	tbsp sugar
2	tbsp lime juice
¹/₃	cup water
	fresh dill for garnish
	banana leaf or aluminum foil for wrapper

▶▶Mix the sugar and salt with water, stir over low heat until sugar has all dissolved. Turn off the heat, allow to cool before adding garlic, hot chili and lime juice, mix thoroughly. Follow with coriander, stirring again to combine.

▶▶Clean the prawns, wrap the whole prawns in banana leaf or foil. Grill over charcoal fire for 8-10 minutes or until just cooked.

▶▶Serve the char-grilled prawns with the spicy sauce and add some personal touch with fresh dill.

Serves 2

step-by-step

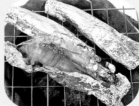

1. Simmer the water, sugar and salt over low heat until the sugar has dissolved and it becomes syrupy.

2. Allow the sauce to cool, then add garlic, hot chili and lime juice. Follow with coriander.

3. Wash the prawns, wrap the whole prawns in banana leaves or aluminum foil.

4. Char-grill over medium heat for 8-10 minutes until done.

grilled prawns in tamarind sauce
[kung yaang sauce makhaam piak]

6	giant fresh water prawns, about 150 grams each
1	tbsp finely chopped coriander root
1/2	cup thinly sliced shallot
1	tbsp chopped garlic
1/4	tsp salt
3	tbsp palm sugar
1 1/2	tbsp fish sauce
4	tbsp tamarind juice
3	tbsp water
1 1/2	tbsp vegetable oil
	coriander leaves for garnish

▶ Prepare tamarind sauce by frying garlic, shallots and coriander roots in oil over medium heat until fragrant. Add palm sugar, tamarind juice, salt, fish sauce and water. Stir well to combine. When the mixture comes to the boil, turn off the heat. Put aside.

▶ Wash the prawns, cut in half lengthwise. Grill the prawns with shell-on until just done, arrange on a serving plate. Pour the tamarind sauce over, and garnish with coriander leaves before serving.

Serves 2

step-by-step

1. Sauté garlic, shallot and coriander roots in oil over medium heat until fragrant.

2. Stir in sugar, tamarind juice, salt, fish sauce and water.

3. When the sauce comes to the boil, turn off the heat. Put aside as the tamarind sauce.

4. Wash the prawns, cut in half lengthwise and split.

stir-fried prawns with tamarind sauce
[kung phat sauce makhaam piak]

500	grams giant fresh water prawn, about 150 grams each
2	tbsp chopped onion
1	red spur chili, shredded
1	tbsp thinly sliced garlic, crisp-fried
2	tbsp thinly sliced shallot, crisp-fried
7	dried hot chilies, crisp-fried
2	tbsp palm sugar
1	tbsp fish sauce
1/3	cup tamarind juice
2	tbsp chicken stock or water
2	tbsp cooking oil
	fresh coriander for garnish

▶▶ Wash the prawns, shell and remove dark veins. Discard the heads but keep the tails intact.

▶▶ Fry chopped onion in oil over medium heat until golden and fragrant, add palm sugar, chicken stock, tamarind juice, and fish sauce, stir well until the sauce thickens. Add the prawns and fry until done. Turn off the heat.

▶▶ Arrange on a serving dish, sprinkle fried garlic, fried shallots, fried chilies and shredded spur chili over. Garnish with fresh coriander and enjoy!

Serves 2-3

step-by-step

1. Wash the prawns, shell and de-vein. Discard the heads but keep the tails intact.

2. Fry chopped onion until golden, add sugar, fish sauce, tamarind juice and chicken stock, stir together until the sauce thickens..

3. Add in the prawns and cook until just done.

4. Transfer to arrange on a serving dish, sprinkle fried garlic, fried shallots, fried dried chilies and red chili on top.

garlic prawns
[kung krathiam]

8-12 giant fresh water prawns
  2 tbsp chopped garlic
  ¼ cup sliced spring onion
  ¼ cup finely chopped ginger
  1 tbsp finely chopped coriander root
  1 tsp pepper
1¼ tsp sugar
  ½ tbsp fish sauce
  ¼ cup vegetable oil
    tips of spring onion for garnish

▸ Wash the prawns, shell and de-vein. Remove the heads but keep the tails intact.

▸ Fry chopped garlic, coriander roots, and pepper in oil over medium heat until fragrant. Add sugar and fish sauce, stir well.

▸ Add the prawns and fry until done. Follow with spring onion and ginger, stir to mix then turn off the heat.

▸ Spoon onto a serving dish, garnish with spring onion tips as a finishing touch.

Serves 4

step-by-step

1. Wash the prawns, shell and de-vein. Remove the heads but keep the tails intact.

2. Sauté garlic, coriander roots and pepper in oil over medium heat until fragrant.

3. Stir in sugar and fish sauce, then add the prawns and sauté until done.

4. Add spring onion and ginger, stir well.

prawns and mung bean noodles in clay pot
[kung op wunsen]

500	grams tiger prawn
1	cup mung bean noodle, soaked and cut into short lengths (from 100 grams dry noodle)
3	slices crushed mature ginger
5	crushed coriander roots
1	onion, finely sliced
1	tbsp crushed peppercorn
$^1/_4$	tsp salt
1	tbsp sugar
2	tbsp light soy sauce
1	tbsp seasoning sauce
1	tbsp oyster sauce
1	tbsp whisky
1	tsp sesame oil
2	tbsp cooking oil
	tips of spring onion (about 3"-4" long) for garnish

▸ Wash the prawns and trim.

▸ Place a wok of oil over medium heat, when the oil is hot, fry coriander roots, ginger, peppercorns and onion until fragrant. Remove from the wok, transfer to a mixing bowl.

▸ Add the noodles and the other ingredients, toss well. Follow with the prawns and toss again.

▸ Transfer to a clay pot, cover with a lid, and place over low heat for 30 minutes until everything is cooked. Remove from the heat. Garnish with spring onion tips. Best when served steaming hot.

Serves 2

step-by-step

1. Sauté coriander roots, ginger, onion and peppercorns over medium heat until fragrant.

2. Add the soaked mung bean noodles and the remaining ingredients, toss to mix well.

3. Add the prawns and toss again.

4. Transfer to a clay pot, cover the lid.

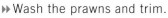

steamed prawns in soy sauce
[kung neung see-iu]

15	giant fresh water prawns, about 100 grams each
1	tbsp finely chopped spring onion
2	coriander roots, finely pounded
2	tbsp finely pounded garlic
1/4	tsp pepper
2	tbsp light soy sauce
1	tbsp oyster sauce
	spring onion tips (about 3"-4" long) for garnish

▸▸ Wash, shell and de-vein the prawns, cut off the head tips but keep the tails intact. Split the prawns for half their length and fold the tails back through the cut. Transfer to a dish, arrange nicely and set aside.

▸▸ Mix the coriander roots, garlic, soy sauce and oyster sauce together, pour over the prawns.

▸▸ Steam the prawns over boiling water on high heat for 5 minutes or until done. Remove from the steamer, sprinkle on top with pepper and spring onion, garnish with spring onion tips as a finishing touch and serve while steaming hot.

Serves 4-5

step-by-step

1. Wash the prawns, shell and de-vein. Cut off the head tips but keep the tails intact. Fold the tails back through the cut.

2. Mix the coriander roots, garlic, soy sauce and oyster sauce together.

3. Pour the mixture over the prawns.

4. Steam the prawns over boiling water on high heat for 5 minutes or until done.

fried stuffed squid
[phat plaa meuk yat sai]

200 grams medium-sized squid
  ½ cup shiitake mushroom, soaked and cut into pieces
  2 tbsp sliced ginger, 1 tsp chopped garlic
  1 tbsp oyster sauce
  ¼ cup water, ¼ cup vegetable oil
     carved chili and spring onion tips for garnish

stuffing
200 grams minced pork
  1 egg, lightly beaten, 1 tbsp chopped onion
  1 tsp minced coriander root
  1 tbsp chopped garlic
  ¼ tsp pepper, 1 tsp sugar
  1 tbsp light soy sauce, 1 tbsp fish sauce

▸▸ Wash the squid well, remove the inedible parts and wash again. Drain and put aside.

▸▸ Mix all the stuffing together and stuff into the squid, be careful not to overfill. Steam over boiling water on high heat for 8 minutes. Remove from the steamer and leave to cool. Cut into rings about 1" thick.

▸▸ Place oil in a wok, add garlic and fry over medium heat until golden and fragrant. Add ginger, shiitake mushrooms, oyster sauce and water, and stir well. Add in the stuffed squid and stir lightly. Arrange on a serving dish. Garnish with red chili and spring onion tips before serving.

Serves 4

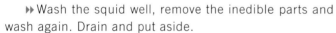
step-by-step

1. Mix the minced pork and other ingredients together to make the stuffing.

2. Fill the pork mixture into the squid and arrange on a plate.

3. Slice the steamed squid into rings about 1" thick.

4. Stir together ginger, shiitake mushrooms, oyster sauce and water with fried garlic. Add the squid and stir well to combine.

stir-fried crab with curry powder
[poo phat phong kari]

- 1 crab, about 500 grams
- 1 tbsp curry powder, 2 eggs
- 1 tbsp chopped garlic
- 1 onion, cut into wedges
- 1 celery, cut into short length about 1½" long
- 1 red spur chili, sliced diagonally
- ½ tsp pepper, ½ cup fresh milk
- 1 tbsp sugar
- 1½ tbsp fish sauce
- 1½ tbsp light soy sauce
- 1 tbsp oyster sauce
- 2 cups water, 2 tbsp cooking oil

▸▸Wash and clean the crab thoroughly, remove the shell and discard the inedible part. Wash again, and cut into big pieces.

▸▸Beat the eggs lightly, mix with fresh milk and put aside.

▸▸Sauté chopped garlic in oil over medium heat until fragrant, put in the crab and turn the heat up to high. Fry for a few minutes, pour in water to cover the crab and put the cover on.

▸▸When only half of the liquid remains, add curry powder and season with sugar, fish sauce, soy sauce and oyster sauce. Add onion, pour in the egg mixture, stirring until the sauce thickens, then add red chili and celery. Turn off the heat. Transfer to a serving dish and serve.

Serves 4-5

step-by-step

1. Remove the crab shell, discard the inedible part.

2. Beat the eggs and fresh milk lightly and put aside.

3. Add the crab, turn the heat up to high. Pour in water to cover the crab.

4. Stir in the egg mixture, stir until thickened. Add chili and celery, then turn off the heat.

stuffed cabbage with beancurd
[kalamplee phan tao hoo]

8	leaves cabbage, 3 pieces soft white beancurd
300	grams minced pork, 1 egg
8	Chinese celery stalks, $1/4$ cup finely chopped garlic
1	tbsp corn flour, 1 tsp salt
$2^{1}/_{2}$	tbsp sugar, 4 tbsp light soy sauce
2	cups chicken stock, 2 tbsp cooking oil
	celery and slices of red spur chili for garnish

▸▸Wash the cabbage leaves well. Place a pot of salted water over medium heat and bring to the boil. Blanch the cabbage leaves in boiling salted water until soft. Remove and drain. Blanch the celery stalks and drain as well.

▸▸Fry minced pork and garlic over medium heat. Break the pork into small bits, season with $1/2$ tbsp sugar and 1 tbsp sauce. When the pork is done, add beancurd, mash into small pieces. Reduce the heat, break in an egg and stir well. Remove from the heat, set aside as the filling.

▸▸Divide the filling into 8 portions, spoon each portion onto the center of a cabbage leave, wrap the leave tightly, tie with the celery stalk.

▸▸Transfer the stuffed cabbage into a pot, add chicken stock and the remaining sugar and soy sauce, simmer for 20 minutes. Mix corn flour with 2 tbsp of water, and stir into the stock. Reduce the heat and continue cooking until the sauce thickens. Turn off the heat.

▸▸Transfer to a serving dish and pour the sauce over the mixture. Garnish with celery and red chili slices as a finishing touch before serving.

Serves 4

step-by-step

1. Fry the minced pork, break up to small pieces. Add the beancurd.

2. Tie the stuffed cabbage with boiled celery stalk.

3. Arrange the stuffed cabbage in a pot, add chicken stock, sugar and soy sauce.

4. Mix corn flour with 2 tbsp of water, and stir into the pot.

stir-fried kale with oyster sauce
[phat khana naam man hawy]

10	medium-sized kale plants
20	straw mushrooms, halved
1	tbsp chopped garlic
1/4	tsp pepper
1/4	tsp salt
1	tsp sugar
4	tbsp oyster sauce
3	tbsp cooking oil

▸▸ Wash the kale thoroughly, peel off old leaves and the tough skin covering the stems.

▸▸ Bring the water to the boil, add 1 tbsp of salt, add the kale and blanch until just done. Transfer to soak in cold water until cool, and drain. Blanch the mushrooms in the same way. Put aside.

▸▸ Heat the oil until hot, add garlic and fry over medium heat until fragrant. Add the kale and mushrooms, stir well. Season with oyster sauce, sugar, pepper and salt. Stir thoroughly, then turn off the heat.

▸▸ Spoon onto a serving dish and serve hot.

Serves 4

step-by-step

1. Discard old leaves and tough outer skin.

2. Blanch the kale in hot boiling water until done, transfer to soak in cold water immediately.

3. Sauté the kale and mushrooms with garlic, stir well.

4. Season with salt, sugar, and oyster sauce. Sprinkle pepper over and stir to combine.

stir-fried bean sprouts and crispy pork

[phat thua ngawk kap moo krawp]

500 grams bean sprout
300 grams crisp-fried pork belly
1 tsp chopped garlic
2 tbsp light soy sauce
3 tbsp cooking oil

crispy pork belly

1 piece (500 grams) pork belly about 4" thick
4 tbsp vinegar
3 tbsp salt
5 cups water
4 cups cooking oil, for deep-frying

» Bring the water to the boil, add 3 tbsp of vinegar and 1 tbsp of salt. Dip the pork belly into the boiling water and boil until the skin is soft. Remove, score the skin in a crisscross pattern and cut in half lengthwise about 2" thick. Rub well with salt and vinegar, leave to cool completely. Deep-fry in hot oil until the skin turns crisp, remove and cut into pieces about $1/2$" thick.

» Sauté the garlic in oil over medium heat until golden and fragrant. Add the pork and bean sprouts, stir quickly. Season with soy sauce, then remove from the heat and serve immediately.

Serves 4

step-by-step

1. Sauté the garlic in oil over medium heat until golden and fragrant.

2. Add the crispy pork belly, stir well.

3. Add bean sprouts and stir-fry quickly.

4. Season with soy sauce, transfer to a serving dish and serve steaming hot.

stir-fried chicken and green eggplant

[phat makheua yao]

2	cups green eggplant, sliced diagonally
300	grams boneless chicken breast, cut into bite-sized pieces
2	red spur chilies, sliced diagonally
1/2	cup sweet basil leaf
1	tbsp chopped garlic
1	tbsp fermented soybean
1	tbsp fish sauce
1	tsp dark soy sauce
1/4	cup chicken stock
2	tbsp cooking oil
	sweet basil sprig for garnish

▸▸ Heat the oil over medium heat until hot, fry chopped garlic until golden. Add the chicken and cook for 5 minutes. Then, add the eggplant and cook for further 5 minutes.

▸▸ Season to taste with fermented soybeans, fish sauce and dark soy sauce, continue cooking for a few minutes. Add chicken stock, chilies and basil leaves, bring to the boil, then remove from the heat. Arrange on a serving dish, garnish with sweet basil and serve.

Serves 4

step-by-step

1. Sauté chicken with fried garlic for 5 minutes.

2. Follow with eggplant, continue cooking for further 5 minutes.

3. Season to taste with fermented soybeans, fish sauce and dark soy sauce. Stir-fry for a few minutes.

4. Add chicken stock, red chilies and sweet basil leaves. Cook until boiling.

stir-fried prawns and vegetables
[phat phak anaamai]

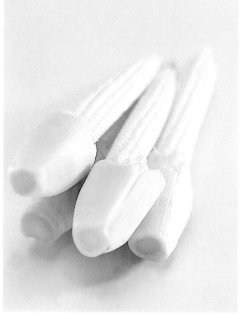

  1 young loofah
10 ears baby corn
10 straw mushrooms
12 giant fresh water prawns, about 100 grams each
  1 tbsp chopped garlic
¼ tsp salt
  3 tbsp oyster sauce
  3 tbsp cooking oil

▸▸Wash the prawns, shell and de-vein. Remove the heads and tails, set aside.

▸▸Wash the loofah, baby corns, and mushrooms. Peel the loofah and slice diagonally into bite-sized pieces. Cut the baby corns into 2 pieces. Trim of the dirt and cut mushrooms in half.

▸▸Heat the oil until hot, fry garlic over medium heat until golden and fragrant. Add the prawns and fry until done. Add the salt and all the vegetables, stir well and cook until everything is done. Season to taste with oyster sauce and stir to blend. Turn off the heat. Transfer to a serving dish. Best when served piping hot.

Serves 4

1. Cut the prawns in half crosswise.

2. Cut the baby corns into 2 pieces, half the mushrooms and slice the loofah diagonally into pieces.

3. Sauté the prawns with fried garlic until just done.

4. Sprinkle with salt, stir well. Then add all the vegetables and cook until tender and done.

red curry with mushrooms
[kaeng phet het]

300	grams straw mushroom
1	tbsp red curry paste (see p. 21)
1¹/₂	cups coconut milk
1	red or green chili, sliced diagonally
3-4	kaffir lime leaves, torn
¹/₂	tbsp palm sugar
3	tbsp fish sauce
¹/₂	cup water or chicken stock
	slices of red and green chilies for garnish

▸▸Wash off the dirt and clean the mushrooms well. Cut in half lengthwise.

▸▸Heat half of the coconut milk over medium heat until a film of oil surfaces, add red curry paste and sauté for 3 minutes until fragrant and red oil surfaces.

▸▸Add the remaining coconut milk and chicken stock, followed by the mushrooms and continue cooking until everything is done. Season with fish sauce and sugar. Sprinkle kaffir lime leaves and chilies, continue cooking until it returns to the boil before removing from heat. Spoon onto a serving dish, garnish with slices of red and green chilies and serve hot.

Serves 4

step-by-step

1. Heat ³/₄ cup of coconut milk over medium heat until the oil surfaces.

2. Stir in the red curry paste, sauté for 3 minutes until fragrant and the red oil surfaces.

3. Add the remaining coconut milk and chicken stock. Follow with the mushrooms.

4. Season with fish sauce and sugar. Sprinkle kaffir lime leaves and chili on top.

minced pork and tomato chili paste
[naam phrik awng]

5   dried red spur chilies, seeded and soaked in water
1   cup sliced cherry tomato
3   tbsp minced pork
1   coriander plant, leaves only
3   tbsp chopped onion
5   cloves garlic
3   cloves chopped garlic
1   tbsp finely sliced galangal
1   tsp salt, 1 tsp shrimp paste
1/2 cup water, 2 tbsp cooking oil
    condiments: pork crackling
    fresh vegetables: cucumber, yard-long beans,
    small eggplants and dill
    boiled vegetables: pumpkin and yard-long beans

▸▸ Put chilies, salt and galangal in a mortar, and pound well. Add onion, shrimp paste and whole garlic cloves, pound thoroughly. Follow with minced pork and tomatoes, pound lightly to mix well after each adding.

▸▸ Sauté chopped garlic in hot oil over medium heat until golden and fragrant, reduce the heat, add the pork mixture. Stir regularly until fragrant and a red film of oil surfaces. Add water, continue cooking until most of the liquid reduces and the chili paste becomes fairly thick. Turn off the heat. Transfer to a serving bowl, garnish with coriander leaves, and serve with pork crackling, par-boiled and fresh vegetables.

Serves 6

step-by-step

1. Pound onion, shrimp paste and garlic with chilies, galangal and salt to a smooth paste.

2. Add minced pork, pound lightly. Follow with tomatoes, pound again to combine.

3. Sauté garlic over medium heat until golden and fragrant. Reduce the heat, add the pounded pork mixture and sauté until red oil surfaces and fragrant.

4. Add water and continue cooking until the liquid reduces and the dip becomes thick. Turn off the heat.

coconut sauce with ham
[lon ham]

1	cup diced ham
1/2	cup fermented glutinous rice
2	cups coconut milk (from 400 grams grated coconut)
6	red spur chilies, cut into short length
1/4	cup coriander leaf
1/4	cup sliced shallot
1/4	tsp salt
1	tbsp palm sugar
2-3	tbsp tamarind juice
	fresh vegetables: winged beans, Chinese cabbage and cucumber

▸▸ Put the coconut milk into a pot, bring to the boil over medium heat. Stir in ham and fermented glutinous rice.

▸▸ Season to taste with salt, tamarind juice and palm sugar, stir well. Follow with shallot and chili. When it returns to the boil, remove from the heat.

▸▸ Transfer to a serving dish, sprinkle fresh coriander on top.

▸▸ Serve with fresh vegetables at your choice.

Serves 4

step-by-step

1. Heat the coconut milk over medium heat until boiling, add diced ham.

2. Follow with the fermented glutinous rice, stir well.

3. Season with salt, tamarind juice and sugar. Stir to mix well.

4. Add shallots and chilies, bring back to the boil then remove from the heat.

pork and prawn fried rice
[khao phat moo kung]

```
  4  cups cooked rice
150  grams pork
150  grams prawn, shelled and de-veined
  2  eggs
  1  onion, cut into wedges
  1  tbsp sugar
  3  tbsp light soy sauce
  2  tbsp tomato ketchup
 1/4 cup cooking oil
     fresh vegetables: cucumber, spring onion, lettuce
     lime wedges, shredded red spur chili
     and coriander leaves for garnish
```

▶▶Wash the pork, cut into small pieces, toss with 1 tbsp of light soy sauce and marinate for 10 minutes.

▶▶Heat the oil in a wok over medium heat until hot, fry onion, pork and prawns until done. Season to taste with tomato ketchup, sugar and soy sauce, stir well. Add the rice and stir to mix thoroughly. Remove from the wok.

▶▶Put 1 tbsp of oil in a wok over medium heat. Break the eggs into the hot oil, stirring until done. Add the fried rice, stir well and turn off the heat.

▶▶Transfer to a serving dish, garnish with red chili, coriander leaves and lime wedges. Serve with cucumber, spring onion and lettuce.

Serves 2-3

step-by-step

1. Toss the pork with 1 tbsp of soy sauce and marinate for 10 minutes.

2. Fry onion, pork and prawns in oil over medium heat until done.

3. Season with tomato ketchup, sugar and soy sauce, add cooked rice and stir well. Then remove from the wok.

4. Fry the eggs with 1 tbsp of oil until done. Toss with the fried rice, then turn off the heat.

rice with chicken in gravy
[khao raat naa kai]

4	cups cooked rice, 400 grams chicken
100	grams chicken liver, 1 onion, cut into wedges
1/2	cup straw mushroom or champignon mushroom
150	grams flowering cabbage, cut into 1" pieces
1/2	cup pineapple, diced, 1 tbsp chopped garlic
1/2	tsp pepper
3	tbsp tapioca flour, mix with 1/4 cup of water
1	tsp sugar, 3 tbsp light soy sauce
2 1/2	cups chicken stock, 2 tbsp cooking oil
	slices of red, green and yellow spur chili
	and coriander leaves for garnish

▸▸ Cut the chicken and livers into small pieces, toss with 1 tbsp of light soy sauce and marinate for 10 minutes.

▸▸ Fry the garlic in oil over medium heat until fragrant and golden. Add chicken and livers, sauté until done. Then, add the onion, mushrooms, flowering cabbage and chicken stock. Season with soy sauce and sugar to taste, follow with pineapple and fry until cooked through. Stir in the tapioca batter, stir constantly until the sauce thickens and is clear. When the sauce comes to the boil, turn off the heat.

▸▸ Arrange 1 cup of the cooked rice on a serving plate, spoon the chicken and some sauce over, sprinkle pepper over the top. Garnish with spur chili and coriander leaves. Serve hot with pickled chili in vinegar (finely slice 3 chilies and add to 1/4 cup of vinegar).

Serves 4

step-by-step

1. Toss chicken and livers in 1 tbsp of soy sauce and leave for 10 minutes.

2. Fry garlic over medium heat until golden and fragrant, add the chicken and livers and sauté until done.

3. Add onion, mushrooms, flowering cabbage and chicken stock.

4. Season with soy sauce and sugar. Add in pineapple and cook until done. Stir the tapioca batter until the sauce thickens and is clear.

chicken rice
[khao man kai]

1¹/₂ cups rice
2 pieces chicken breast or thigh
2 crushed coriander roots
10 cloves roughly crushed garlic
1 tsp salt
3 cups water
3 tbsp cooking oil
    fresh vegetables: cucumber,
    spring onion
    lettuce and fresh dill for garnish

soybean sauce
1 hot chili, finely chopped
1 tbsp mature ginger, finely chopped
3 tbsp fermented soybean
1 tsp sugar
1 tbsp vinegar
1 tsp dark soy sauce

▸▸ Strain the fermented soybeans and reserve the liquid. Pound the soybeans thoroughly, then mix with reserved liquid. Season with dark soy sauce, vinegar and sugar to taste. Add ginger and chili, stirring well. Dip into a sauce dish, and serve with the chicken rice.

▸▸ Place the chicken in a pot, add water, salt and coriander roots, cook over low heat until done. Skim off any froth to get the clear broth. Remove the chicken, de-bone and cut into slices. Strain the broth and set aside.

▸▸ Wash the rice, drain and set aside.

▸▸ Heat the oil in a wok, sauté garlic over medium heat until fragrant and golden. Add the rice, stirring well and cook for 3 minutes. Transfer to an electric rice cooker, pour 2¹/₂ cups of chicken broth over the rice and cook until the rice is done.

▸▸ Spoon the rice onto a serving dish, arrange the chicken slices on top or at the side, garnish with lettuce and fresh dill. Serve with soybean sauce, sliced cucumbers and spring onion.

Serves 3

step-by-step

1. Mix all ingredients for the sauce, stir together.

2. Occasionally skim off any froth to get the clear broth.

3. Cook the rice with fried garlic over medium heat for 3 minutes.

4. Transfer the rice to an electric rice cooker, add 2¹/₂ cups chicken broth and cook until done.

fried rice with shrimp paste
[khao khluk kapi]

3 cups cooked rice
1 tbsp shrimp paste
3 tbsp fried dried shrimp
1 lightly beaten egg
3 tbsp shallot, finely sliced
1 tbsp chopped garlic
1 tsp sugar
1 tbsp fish sauce
1 tbsp water
1/2 cup cooking oil
   condiments: wedges of lime,
   spring onion
   hot chili slices and coriander
   leaves for garnish

sweet pork

1 cup pork, sliced into small pieces
1 tbsp chopped shallot
2 tbsp palm sugar
1 tbsp fish sauce
1 tsp dark soy sauce
1/4 cup water
2 tbsp cooking oil

▶ To make the sweet pork: Sauté shallot in oil over medium heat until golden and fragrant. Add pork and sauté until it turns white. Season with fish sauce, dark soy sauce and sugar, stir well. Follow with water. Simmer until dry and the pork looks glossy. Remove from the heat.

▶ Fry garlic in oil over medium heat until fragrant, mix shrimp paste and water together, pour into the wok and stir well. Season with sugar and fish sauce, reduce the heat. Add the rice, stir thoroughly to mix well. Transfer to a dish.

▶ Heat 1 tbsp of oil over low heat, spread to cover the sides of the wok. Pour in the beaten egg and spread to obtain a thin omelette. When the egg is done, remove from the heat, roll up and cut into thin strips.

▶ Spoon the fried rice onto a serving dish, arrange the omelette, sweet pork, fried shrimps and sliced shallots nicely. Garnish with coriander and chili as a finishing touch, and serve with spring onion and lime wedges.

Serves 2

step-by-step

1. Fry the pork in the seasoning until dry and looks glossy, remove and put aside.

2. Mix the shrimp paste with water, and add to the fried garlic, stir well.

3. Season the shrimp paste mixture with sugar and fish sauce. Add the rice and stir to combine, then remove from the heat.

4. Swirl the egg to obtain the thin omelette.

rice with chinese sausages
[khao op kun chiang]

2	cups rice, 2 Chinese sausages *(kun chiang)*
100	grams pork tenderloin, 200 grams prawn
3	shiitake mushrooms, soaked and sliced
¼	cup thinly sliced ginger
2	tbsp finely sliced spring onion
1½	tbsp chopped garlic, 2 tbsp oyster sauce
2	tbsp light soy sauce, 4 tbsp cooking oil
4	spring onions

▶ Slice the sausages and pork into bite-sized pieces. Wash the prawns, shell and de-vein, remove the heads but keep the tails intact.

▶ Wash the rice and drain.

▶ Fry garlic and ginger in oil over medium heat until fragrant, add sausages, pork, and prawns. Fry until everything is done, add mushrooms, stirring well. Follow with the rice. Season to taste with oyster sauce and soy sauce, stir to mix well. Then, transfer to an electric rice cooker.

▶ Add plain water to the water in which mushrooms were soaked to obtain a total of 3 cups, add to the fried rice and cook until done.

▶ Spoon the rice onto a serving dish, sprinkle sliced spring onion over the top. And serve with fresh spring onion.

Serves 4

step-by-step

1. Slice the Chinese sausages and pork into pieces. Wash the prawns, shell and de-vein, remove the heads but keep the tails intact.

2. Fry chopped garlic and ginger in oil over medium heat until fragrant, add sausages, pork and prawns, stir until everything is done.

3. Add mushrooms and stir well. Follow with the rice, season with oyster sauce and soy sauce. Stir to mix well.

4. Transfer the fried rice to an electric rice cooker, pour in water and the water which mushrooms are soaked. Cook until the rice is done.

thai-style fried noodles
[phat thai]

4 cups thin rice noodle,
  soaked for 3 minutes
50 grams pork, cut into small pieces
3 eggs
1 piece beancurd, diced
250 grams bean sprout
50 grams Chinese chives,
  cut into short length
1 tbsp chopped shallot
1 tbsp chopped garlic
3 tbsp chopped salted
  Chinese radish
1 tsp chili powder
1/2 cup ground roasted peanut
4 tbsp sugar
3 tbsp fish sauce
4 tbsp tamarind juice or vinegar
1/4 cup water
8 tbsp cooking oil
  fresh vegetables: bean sprouts,
  Chinese chives, banana bud,
  Indian pennyworth and wedges of
  lime

▶▶ Fry shallot and garlic in 3 tbsp of oil over medium heat until fragrant. Add noodles and water, stir until tender. Season with sugar, fish sauce and tamarind juice. Stir well, then push the noodles to the side of the wok.

▶▶ Add 3 tbsp of oil to the same wok, add pork, salted Chinese radish, beancurd and chili powder. Sauté until the pork is done, toss well with the fried noodles, then push the mixture back to the side of the wok again.

▶▶ Put 2 tbsp of oil into the wok, break the eggs in and stir until done. Toss again with the noodles, add the bean sprouts and Chinese chives. Stir until everything is done.

▶▶ Transfer to a serving dish, sprinkle roasted peanuts on top. Serve with fresh vegetables.

Serves 4

Tip: _A lot of oil is specified for this recipe, but do not add all at one time. Add a little at a time when the noodles are dry. It is not necessary to use up all the oil in the recipe._

step-by-step

1. Sauté garlic and shallot over medium heat until golden and fragrant, then add the rice noodles.

2. Fry until the noodles are tender, season with sugar, fish sauce and tamarind juice. Stir well, scrape onto the side of the wok.

3. Fry the pork, salted radish, beancurd and chili powder in 3 tbsp of oil until the pork is done. Toss well with the fried noodles.

4. Break the eggs in 2 tbsp of oil, stir until done, toss again with the noodles.

fried noodles with prawns
[sen jan phat kung]

4	cups thin rice noodle (Chanthaburi dried rice noodle), soaked for 3 minutes
8-10	prawns, shelled and de-veined
50	grams bean sprout
100	grams Chinese chives
5	dried spur chilies, seeded and soaked in water
2	tbsp sliced shallot
2	tbsp chopped garlic
$^1/_4$	tsp salt
$^1/_4$	cup palm sugar
$^1/_4$	cup fish sauce
$^1/_4$	cup tamarind juice
$^1/_4$	cup cooking oil
	fresh vegetables: wedges of lime, Chinese chives, bean sprouts

▶ Pound the dried chilies and salt well, add garlic and shallots, pound thoroughly to obtain a smooth paste.

▶ Sauté the chili paste in oil over medium heat until fragrant. Season to taste with palm sugar, fish sauce and tamarind juice. Add the prawns, and stir regularly until done.

▶ Add noodles, continue cooking for a few minutes before adding the bean sprouts and Chinese chives and mix well. When everything is done, turn off the heat.

▶ Arrange on a serving dish and serve with fresh vegetables.

Serves 4

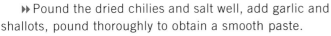
step-by-step

1. Pound dried chilies and salt together well, follow with shallots and garlic.

2. Sauté the chili mixture in oil over medium heat until fragrant.

3. Season with sugar, fish sauce and tamarind juice. Then add the prawns, and fry until done.

4. Add the noodles, fry for a few minutes. Add bean sprouts and Chinese chives, stir until everything is done. Turn off the heat.

crispy fried noodles
[mee krawp]

150 grams rice vermicelli
¼ cup minced pork , ¼ cup minced prawn
1 piece yellow beancurd, finely sliced about a
    matchstick-sized and crisp-fried
1 tbsp garlic and shallot, chopped
2 bulbs pickled garlic, thinly sliced
1 shredded red spur chili
1 coriander plant, leaves only
1 tbsp fermented soybean
1 tbsp vinegar, 1 tbsp fish sauce
4 tbsp palm sugar, 1 tsp powder chili
1 tbsp lime juice, 1 tbsp shredded kaffir lime leaf
3 cups cooking oil
    fresh vegetables: bean sprouts, Chinese chives

▶▶Soak the rice vermicelli for 12-15 minutes until soft, drain. Fry in hot oil, a little at a time, until crisp and lightly golden. Remove and drain. Continue frying until finished.

▶▶Heat ¼ cup of oil in a pan, sauté garlic and shallots until fragrant, add pork and prawns. Season with fermented soybeans, vinegar, fish sauce, palm sugar and chili powder. When it begins to dry, add lime juice. The taste should be sweet, sour and salty.

▶▶Reduce the heat, add fried rice vermicelli. Toss until well-coated, then add fried beancurd, toss thoroughly and spoon onto a serving dish. Top with pickled garlic, kaffir lime leaves, coriander and chili. Serve with fresh vegetables.

Serves 6

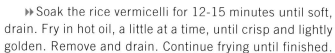
step-by-step

1. Fry the soaked rice vermicelli in hot oil, a little at a time, until golden crispy. Remove from the oil and drain.

2. Sauté garlic and shallot over medium heat until fragrant.

3. Add minced pork and prawn, stir to combine.

4. Add fried beancurd as the last ingredient, toss again to mix well.

fermented rice vermicelli with fish curry sauce

[khanom jeen naam yaa]

1 kilogram fermented rice vermicelli
$^1/_2$ cup coconut cream
5 cups coconut milk
200 grams white meaty fish
2-3 tbsp fish sauce
2 hard-boiled eggs
1 cup boiled bitter gourd,
 seeded and finely sliced
$^1/_2$ cup sliced cucumber
$^1/_2$ cup yard-long bean,
 cut into short lengths and boiled
$^1/_2$ cup shredded cabbage
$^1/_2$ cup blanched bean sprout
1 cup hairy basil leaf

curry paste

3 dried chilies, seeded and
 soaked in water
1 piece grilled salted fish,
 about 1" thick
$^1/_4$ cup sliced shallot
3 tbsp sliced garlic
2 tsp finely sliced galangal
2 tbsp sliced lemon grass
1 cup sliced wild ginger *(krachai)*
1 tsp salt, 1 cup water
1 tsp shrimp paste
 finely sliced red chili for garnish

▶▶ Put all the ingredients for the curry in a pot of water, cook until tender and done. Remove from the heat, allow to cool, then pound or blend thoroughly.

▶▶ Cook the fish meat in 1 cup of boiling water until done. Remove, and set aside the broth. Blend the fish with the curry paste.

▶▶ Place coconut milk in pot over low heat and bring to the boil. Pour in the fish broth and season with fish sauce. Add the curry mixture, stir regularly. Simmer until the curry thickens and becomes fragrant and a red film of oil surfaces. Add coconut cream, stir well and cook until boiling. Remove from the heat.

▶▶ Arrange the fermented rice vermicelli on a serving dish, and serve with the hot fish curry sauce, boiled eggs and vegetables.

Serves 5

step-by-step

1. Cook the ingredients for the curry over medium heat until tender.

2. Blend the cooked fish with the curry paste finely.

3. Add the curry mixture into a pot of coconut milk after seasoning with fish sauce.

4. When the curry becomes thicken and the red oil surfaces, pour in the coconut cream.

fermented rice vermicelli in peanut chili sauce

[khanom jeen naam phrik]

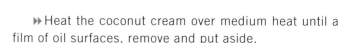

400	grams fermented rice vermicelli
1	cup coconut cream
2³/₄	cups coconut milk
400	grams prawn, shelled and de-veined
50	grams ground roasted hulled mung bean
¹/₄	cup coriander leaf
2	tbsp chopped garlic
1	tbsp chili powder
¹/₄	cup fried dried hot chili
3	sliced roasted shallots
2	tbsp sliced roasted garlic
1	tsp sliced roasted galangal
1	tbsp finely sliced coriander root
6	tbsp palm sugar
6	tbsp fish sauce
6	tbsp lime juice
¹/₄	cup cooking oil
	condiments: sliced boiled Thai convolvulus and yard-long beans, thinly sliced banana flower soaked in lime water

▸▸ Pound roasted shallots, roasted garlic, galangal and coriander root together.

▸▸ Heat the coconut cream over medium heat until a film of oil surfaces, remove and put aside.

▸▸ Cook the prawns in the coconut milk over medium heat until just done. Remove the prawns with a slotted spoon, mince or pound finely. Set aside.

▸▸ Combine the coconut cream and milk together gradually spoon into the pot of cooked prawns until all the liquid is used up. Stir to combine. Add mung beans and pounded garlic paste, stir to mix well. Season to taste with fish sauce, sugar and lime juice. The taste should be sweet, sour and salty. Turn off the heat and put aside.

▸▸ Sauté the garlic in oil over medium heat until golden and fragrant, remove from the oil. Fry chili powder over low heat until the oil turns red, then pour into the prawn sauce. Sprinkle coriander leaves and fried garlic on top.

▸▸ To serve: Arrange the fermented rice vermicelli and the condiments on a plate, spoon ¹/₂ cup of the sauce over. Serve with fried dried hot chilies.

Serves 6

step-by-step

1. Pound roasted shallots, roasted garlic, galangal and coriander roots together well.

2. Pound the cooked prawns finely.

3. Mix the coconut cream, coconut milk and prawn. Add in the ground mung beans and garlic paste, stir well.

4. Fry chili powder over low heat until the oil is red. Transfer to the prawn sauce, add coriander and fried garlic.

bananas in coconut milk
[kluay buat chee]

10	nearly ripe *naam waa* bananas
¹/₂	cup coconut cream
3	cups coconut milk
1	cup sugar
1	tsp salt

▸▸ Peel the bananas, cut each in half lengthwise, then cut across to get 4 pieces.

▸▸ Pour the coconut milk into a pot, and cook over medium heat until it boils. Add the bananas, and cook until soft, then add sugar and salt.

▸▸ After sugar has completely dissolved, pour in the coconut cream, then remove from the heat. Serve the warm bananas in a dessert bowl.

Serves 5-6

step-by-step

1. Cut each bananas in half lengthwise, and cut across to get 4 pieces.

2. Add the bananas into the hot boiling coconut milk.

3. When they are done, add salt and sugar.

4. Add the coconut cream after the sugar has all dissolved.

corn pudding
[khao phoht piak]

3	cups corn, thinly slice all the kernels
2	cups water
1	cup sugar
$1/4$	cup tapioca flour
1	cup coconut cream
$1^1/_2$	tsp salt

▸▸ Bring the water to the boil over medium heat, put in the corn kernels and stir frequently until cooked through. Add the sugar and continue to boil until completely dissolved.

▸▸ Mix the flour with some water, and add to the corn. Continue cooking and stir regularly until the flour is done, thick and clear, remove from the heat.

▸▸ Mix the coconut cream and salt together, bring to the boil over low heat, then remove from the heat. Serve the sweet corn and top with some of the salted coconut cream.

Serves 5-6

Tip: *Tapioca flour can be substituted by corn flour.*

1. Cook the corn kernels until done.

2. Add sugar into the corn, and stir until completely dissolved.

3. Mix tapioca flour with water, and pour into the pot.

4. Mix the coconut cream with salt, bring to the boil over low heat.

step-by-step

rice balls with poached eggs in coconut milk

[bua lawy khai waan]

1. Knead the flour with water until soft.

1	cup glutinous rice flour
4	eggs, 1 cup sugar
1	cup coconut cream, heat until hot
$^1/_4$	cup water for kneading
$2^1/_2$	cups water

2. Roll the dough into small balls about 1 cm in diameter.

▸▸ Knead the glutinous rice flour with water until a dough forms. Shape into small balls about 1 cm in diameter. Continue shaping until finished.

▸▸ Bring the water to the boil over medium heat, drop the balls in boiling water, and boil until done (they will float to the surface). Remove with a slotted spoon, and place in cold water until slightly cool, remove and drain.

▸▸ Combine sugar with $^1/_2$ cups of water, and bring to the boil. When all the sugar has dissolved, strain and bring back to the boil. Break the eggs into the bowl and carefully drop into the hot syrup. Boil for a while, then turn the eggs over and continue boiling for a little while. Spoon a poached egg into a bowl, add the rice balls and some syrup. Top with coconut cream, serve hot.

Serves 3-4

3. Cook the balls in hot boiling water until done, transfer to soak in cold water.

Tip: The **rice balls with poached eggs in coconut milk** *will be more aromatic if the jasmine-flavored water is used instead of water.*

4. Use a ladle to turn the eggs softly.

mock pomegranate seeds in coconut ice syrup

[thap thim krawp]

1. Toss the water chestnuts well with red liquid.

1	cup canned water chestnut, cut into small cubes
$^1/_2$	cup tapioca flour
150	grams sugar
$^3/_4$	cup coconut milk
$^3/_4$	cup water
	red food coloring, crushed ice

➤➤ Mix the food coloring with some water, soak the water chestnut for 10 minutes, drain and coat with tapioca flour. Shake off any excess flour.

➤➤ Bring water to the boil, put in the floured water chestnut. Boil until they float to the surface, remove with a slotted spoon and drop in cold water. Drain and wrap in a cheesecloth.

➤➤ Combine the sugar and water in a pot, boil over medium heat until it becomes syrupy. Add the coconut milk and stir to combine. Remove from the heat.

➤➤ Mix 3 tablespoons of the boiled water chestnut or the mock pomegranate seeds with sufficient amount of coconut syrup and some crushed ice.

Serves 3

Tip: *Tapioca flour can be substituted by corn flour.*

2. Toss the red water chestnuts with tapioca flour until well-coated.

3. Shake off any excess flour.

4. Boil in hot boiling water until done and floated to the surface. Transfer to soak in cold water.

step-by-step

pumpkin in coconut milk
[fak thawng kaeng buat]

1 kilogram ripe pumpkin
1 cup coconut cream
4 cups coconut milk
1 cup sugar
$^1/_2$ tsp salt
6 cups clear slaked lime water

▸▸Clean the pumpkin well and peel off the skin. Cut the pumpkin into wedge-shaped and remove the seeds, cut into 1x3 cm pieces. Soak in slaked lime water for 30 minutes.

▸▸Mix the sugar, salt, and coconut milk and cook over medium heat. When the sugar has dissolved, strain and return to the boil. Add the pumpkin and cook until done.

▸▸Pour in the coconut cream and bring back to the boil, then remove from the heat. Spoon into a dessert bowl and serve. Can be served hot or cold.

Serves 5-6

Tip: _If the pumpkin is not soaked in slaked lime water, its texture will be soft and the coconut cream will be quite thick._

1. Remove the seeds.

2. Cut into pieces.

3. Cook pumpkin in the coconut milk until done.

4. Add coconut cream when the pumpkin is done, bring back to the boil.

step-by-step

mung bean balls in coconut milk
[khanom bua lawy thua khiaw]

$^1/_2$ cup glutinous rice flour, $^1/_3$ cup hulled mung bean

2 cups coconut milk, $^1/_4$ tsp salt

$^1/_2$ cup palm sugar

$^1/_4$ cup water

▸▸ Wash the mung beans, soak in warm water for 3 hours. Drain and steam until cooked through. Remove from the heat and mash well.

▸▸ Mix half of the coconut milk with sugar and salt, stir constantly until boiling to prevent any lumps forming, remove from the heat.

▸▸ Combine glutinous rice flour and mashed mung beans together. Gradually add water a little at a time, knead until the mixture becomes soft enough for shaping. Roll into small balls about $^1/_2$" in diameter. Continue shaping until finished.

▸▸ Bring the water to the boil over high heat, drop the bean balls and cook until done—they will float to the surface. Transfer with a slotted spoon to soak in the prepared coconut milk. Place the pot of the prepared coconut milk over the heat, bring to the boil. Add the remaining coconut milk, cook until boiling. Remove from the heat.

Serves 2-3

1. Steam the mung beans until cooked through, mash finely.

2. Mix half of the coconut milk with palm sugar and salt, bring to the boil.

3. Roll the dough into small balls about $^1/_2$" in diameter.

4. Add the remaining coconut milk into the sweets, bring back to the boil and remove from the heat.

step-by-step

tapioca pearl steamed cake
[ta koh saakhoo]

2^1/$_2$ cups small tapioca pearl
3^1/$_4$ cups water
1 cup sugar
15 cups made from banana leaf about 1^1/$_2$" in diameter
    rose petals for garnish

topping

2 cups coconut cream
^{1}/$_4$ cup rice flour
1 tsp salt
2 tsp sugar

▸▸ Wash and drain the tapioca pearls.

▸▸ Bring the water to the boil over medium heat, put in tapioca pearls and sugar, stir well. Boil for 20 minutes until the tapioca pearls are cooked through and transparent. Fill half of the cups with the sweet tapioca pearls.

▸▸ Mix all ingredients for the topping together, stir thoroughly over medium-low heat until thickened. Turn off the heat, fill the remaining half of the cups with the topping. Garnish with rose petals.

15 cups

1. Wash the tapioca pearls, and drain.

2. Bring the water to the boil over medium heat, add sugar and tapioca pearls, stir well.

3. Fill half of each cup with the sweet tapioca pearls, continue until finished.

4. Spoon the coconut topping into the cups until full.

step-by-step

black beans in coconut milk
[thua dam kaeng buat]

1	cup black bean
2¹/₂	cups coconut milk
1	cup palm sugar
¹/₄	tsp salt

▶▶ Soak the black beans for 3 hours or leave overnight. Boil until tender, drain and put aside.

▶▶ Mix the coconut milk with salt and sugar, stir until dissolved. Bring to the boil over medium heat.

▶▶ Add the cooked black beans, continue cooking until boiling well, remove from the heat.

Serves 4

1. Cook the black beans in hot water until done and tender.

2. Mix the coconut milk, salt and sugar, stir until dissolved.

3. Add the cooked black beans.

4. Cook until boiling well, remove from the heat.

mung beans in sugar syrup
[thua khiaw tom naam taan]

1 cup mung bean
1 cup sugar or brown sugar
5 cups water

▸▸Discard bad beans. Wash the beans and soak in warm water for 3 hours or leave overnight. Wash again and drain before using.

▸▸Pour the water into a pot, put in the mung beans, and cook over medium heat until done and tender.

▸▸Add sugar, and stir until completely dissolved. Bring back to the boil, then remove from the heat. Best when serve hot.

<u>Serves 3-4</u>

1. Soak the mung beans in warm water for 3 hours or leave overnight.

2. Drain from water and put aside.

3. Cook the soaked mung beans until done and tender.

4. Add sugar and stir well.

step-by-step

sweet potatoes in ginger syrup
[man tom khing]

500	grams sweet potato
1	cup sugar
4-5	mature ginger slices
4	cups water

▸▸ Peel the potatoes, wash thoroughly, and cut into pieces, then soak in the water.

▸▸ Bring the water to the boil, and put in the sweet potato. When the water returns to the boil once again, add the ginger, and continue cooking until the potato is tender and cooked through.

▸▸ Add sugar, and allow it to dissolve completely, then remove from the heat. Serve hot.

Serves 3-4

1. Cut the sweet potatoes into big pieces, soak in water.

2. Add the sweet potatoes into hot boiling water.

3. Add ginger slices into the boiling sweet potatoes.

4. When the sweet potatoes are done, add sugar and boil until dissolved.

step-by-step

pandanus rice balls

[khanom tom bai toei]

1 cup glutinous rice flour, 2 tbsp coconut cream
100 grams white grated coconut (for the filling)
1 cup white grated coconut (for the coating)
$^{1}/_{2}$ cup sugar, $^{1}/_{8}$ tsp salt
$^{1}/_{4}$ cup thick pandanus juice
special utensil: a brass wok

▸▸ To make the filling: Mix grated coconut and sugar in a brass wok, and cook over medium heat. Stir constantly until thick, remove from the heat. Allow to cool slightly, roll into balls about 1 cm in diameter.

▸▸ Mix 1 cup of grated coconut and salt together, steam over boiling water until hot and set aside.

▸▸ Knead the glutinous rice flour, coconut cream, and pandanus juice together to make a dough, set aside.

▸▸ Roll the dough into small balls about $^{1}/_{2}$" in diameter, flatten each ball and fill with the coconut filling. Wrap the dough to cover the filling completely. Boil the pandanus balls in boiling water over medium-low heat. When they float to the surface, remove with a slotted spoon, and toss in the steamed grated coconut. Arrange on a plate and serve.

Serves 5-6

1. Roll the candied coconut into small balls about 1 cm in diameter.

2. Knead the glutinous rice flour with coconut cream and pandanus juice until a soft dough is formed.

3. Roll the dough into small balls about $^{1}/_{2}$ inches in diameter.

4. Flatten the dough, place a candied coconut ball in the middle and re-roll to completely seal the filling.

step-by-step

chandals in coconut ice syrup
[lawt chawng singapore]

1 cup tapioca flour, ¹/₂ cup hulled mung bean
¹/₄ cup hot boiling water
2 tbsp thick pandanus juice
(or ¹/₄ tsp green food coloring)

sweet coconut milk

¹/₂ cup water or jasmine-flavored water
1 cup sugar, 1 cup coconut milk

▸▸ To make the sweet coconut milk: Mix sugar with jasmine-flavored water, bring to the boil over medium heat. When sugar has dissolved, remove from the heat and leave to cool. Add coconut milk, stir well.

▸▸ Wash the mung beans, soak in warm water for 3 hours. Drain and steam until cooked through. Remove from the heat and mash finely.

▸▸ Mix the mashed beans with tapioca flour, stir in pandanus juice and hot boiling water. The dough will partly be done and clear. Stir thoroughly with a wooden paddle, knead to obtain a soft and smooth dough. Roll the dough into a thin sheet, then cut into long strips.

▸▸ Bring a pot of water to the boil over high heat, cook the dough in boiling water until it floats to the surface. Transfer to soak in cold water and drain. Dip the cooked chandals into the prepared coconut milk. To serve—spoon the chandals and a generous amount of the coconut milk into a serving bowl, top with crushed ice and serve at once.

Serves 4

1. Mix sugar with jasmine-flavored water, bring to the boil.

2. Knead the mashed beans with tapioca flour until it becomes a soft and smooth dough.

3. Roll the dough into thin sheet, then cut into long strips.

4. Cook the chandals in hot boiling water over high heat until they float to the surface and done. Transfer to soak in cold water.

step-by-step

thai banana fritters
[kluay khaek]

10 *naam waa* bananas
¹/₂ cup grated coconut
³/₄ cup rice flour, ¹/₄ cup tapioca flour
¹/₄ cup hulled sesame seed
1 tsp salt, 2 tbsp sugar
1-1¹/₄ cups water
3 cups cooking oil

Mix both kinds of flour with water, sugar, salt, sesame seeds and grated coconut. Stir until thoroughly mixed to obtain a fairly thick batter and no lump remains.

Peel the bananas, slice each lengthwise into 3-4 slices.

Heat the oil in a deep pan over high heat, when the oil is hot, dip the banana slices in the batter and fry until golden brown. Remove and drain.

Serves 5

Tip: *The bananas should be just ripened. Sweet potato and taro can be used as well.*

1. Stir the batter thoroughly until no lump remains and the batter is thick enough to coat the banana.

2. Peel the bananas, slice each lengthwise to get 3-4 slices.

3. Dip the banana slices in the batter and deep-fry in hot oil.

4. Fry until golden crispy, remove and drain.

step-by-step

glutinous rice with banana
[khao tom mat]

1 kilogram glutinous rice
10 ripe *naam waa* bananas
1 cup cooked black bean
2 cups coconut milk
2 tbsp salt
¹/₂ cup sugar
   banana leaves, bamboo strips

▸▸Soak the glutinous rice overnight. Wash and drain before using.

▸▸Dissolve sugar and salt in the coconut milk, strain and put into a pot. Add rice, stir constantly over low heat until dry. Turn off the heat.

▸▸Peel bananas, cut each in half lengthwise.

▸▸Tear the banana leaf into pieces about 7-8" wide. Lay in pairs so that the midrib side of one is opposite that of the other. Spread some rice in the center, place a slice of banana on the rice, cover with more rice, press several black beans into the rice, then wrap the leaf closely. Tie the packet with bamboo strip, and steam over boiling water on high heat for 40-45 minutes until the rice is cooked through. Remove from the steamer.

(20 pieces)

Tip: *If the rice has not been soaked, wrap and tie the packet securely and boil in hot boiling water for 1 hour.*

1. Stir the soaked glutinous rice with coconut milk, salt and sugar until it becomes fairy dry.

2. Peel the bananas, cut in half lengthwise.

3. Spread the glutinous rice in the center, place a piece of banana on the rice.

4. Tie with the bamboo string tightly.

step-by-step

candied-cassava
[man sampalang cheuam]

1	kilogram cassava root
2½	cups sugar
4	cups water
1	cup coconut cream
½	tsp salt
	special utensil: a brass wok

▸▸ Peel the cassava roots and cut into 3" pieces, wash thoroughly.

▸▸ Mix the sugar and water in a brass wok, place over medium heat. When the mixture boils, and all the sugar has dissolved, strain through cheesecloth and bring back to the heat. When the syrup returns to boil once again, reduce the heat. Put in the cassava and boil until cooked through. The flesh will be clear and absorb most of the syrup. Turn off the heat.

▸▸ Mix the coconut cream and salt together, bring to the boil, then remove from the heat. Serve the candied-cassava and spoon the salted coconut cream on top.

Serves 3-4

1. Cut the unpeeled cassava into pieces about 3" long.

2. Peel the cassava

3. Cook the cassava in hot boiling syrup.

4. Cook until the cassava is done and absorb some of the syrup.

step-by-step

mung beans thai custard
[khanom maw kaeng]

4	eggs
2	duck's eggs
¹/₂	cup cooked taro or hulled mung bean, mashed finely
1	cup coconut cream
1	cup palm sugar
¹/₄	cup crisp-fried shallot slice
2	tbsp oil from the fried shallot
3	pandanus leaves
	special utensil: an 8"x8" baking pan, cheesecloth

▸▸ Break all the eggs into a bowl, add sugar and coconut cream. Mix thoroughly by kneading with the pandanus leaves until the sugar has dissolved. Strain the mixture through cheesecloth, add mashed taro or mung beans, and mix well. Pour into an 8"x8" baking pan.

▸▸ Put the oil from the fried shallots into a wok and place over low heat. Pour the mixture in and stir regularly until it becomes thicken, remove from the heat. Transfer to the baking pan and spread out evenly.

▸▸ Bake in an oven at 350ºF for 30 minutes or until the custard is done and the surface is golden brown. Remove from the oven, and allow to cool. Sprinkle with the crisp-fried shallot, and cut into 2"x2" pieces to serve.

Seves 4

1. Mix the eggs, palm sugar and coconut cream by kneading with pandanus leaves.

2. Add the mashed hulled mung beans and stir well.

3. Pour the mixture into a brass wok and stir until it becomes thicken.

4. Pour into a baking pan, spread evenly and bake until done.

step-by-step